"I had the pleasure of meeting William Barr just a few months ago, and I was extremely impressed with his business model and the way he ran his business. Bill has given many people the opportunity to start a new business, and he has changed many lives. Bill has shown that life is about more than just making money and has built a great organization that I feel will continue to grow and prosper."

—**Rodney Webb,** *president,*
CEO, Rodney Webb, LLC

"When I met Bill Barr, I didn't have two pennies to rub together. Two years later from his guidance, I've grown my business 1600 percent, and I'm unstoppable. He has taught me to take my dreams, turn them into goals, and make them a reality. Listen to what he says and implement it immediately. You won't regret it."

—**Mike Clum,** *president,*
Clum Creative Media

"In all of my years of experience in the home improvement industry, I have never met a more dynamic business owner, entrepreneur, or sales trainer than Bill Barr. The system that Bill has created has proven to be more successful than any dealership opportunity that I have witnessed! In just a short time, Bill has established his brand and built a legacy that will last for decades to come."

—**Mike Redman,** director of sales,
TEMO Sunrooms

SELLING
with
PURPOSE

SELLING
—— with ——
PURPOSE
THE UNIVERSAL WAY

WILLIAM H. BARR III

Advantage®

Published by Advantage, Charleston, South Carolina.
Member of Advantage Media Group.

ADVANTAGE is a registered trademark and the Advantage colophon is a trademark of Advantage Media Group, Inc.

Printed in the United States of America.

ISBN: 978-1-59932-671-9
LCCN: 2015957489

This publication is designed to provide accurate and authoritative information in regard to the subject matter covered. It is sold with the understanding that the publisher is not engaged in rendering legal, accounting, or other professional services. If legal advice or other expert assistance is required, the services of a competent professional person should be sought.

Advantage Media Group is proud to be a part of the Tree Neutral® program. Tree Neutral offsets the number of trees consumed in the production and printing of this book by taking proactive steps such as planting trees in direct proportion to the number of trees used to print books. To learn more about Tree Neutral, please visit **www.treeneutral.com**. To learn more about Advantage's commitment to being a responsible steward of the environment, please visit **www.advantagefamily.com/green**

Advantage Media Group is a publisher of business, self-improvement, and professional development books and online learning. We help entrepreneurs, business leaders, and professionals share their Stories, Passion, and Knowledge to help others Learn & Grow. Do you have a manuscript or book idea that you would like us to consider for publishing? Please visit **advantagefamily.com** or call **1.866.775.1696**.

This book is dedicated to the greatest salesman I have ever known, my father, Bill Barr Jr. The lessons he taught me about life and selling shaped my entrepreneurial destiny. He was not only an excellent teacher, he was also a great friend. Dad, I miss you.

TABLE OF CONTENTS

FOREWORD

One of *Merriam–Webster's* definitions of selling is "to persuade or influence to a course of action or to the acceptance of something."

Professional selling is a science! There is no such thing as a born salesperson or a born leader, for that matter. This may sound provocative because of your individual exposure to selling and your interpretation of what selling is. Sure, there are innate behavior characteristic of some people—those with gregarious, outgoing personalities—that make selling or leading seem easier. But no matter the anomalies or short-term success stories we have all heard, the truth is: selling is *taught!* Leadership is *taught!* More importantly, professional selling skills and leadership skills are learned, and with that knowledge and acceptance, "purpose" is developed.

William Barr was introduced to this concept by his Father at an early age, and later in life he began to understand it and accept it. In his early years of selling he was exposed to a structured-step selling system that put the customer first. William knew that understanding the consumer's value system, identifying what was important to the consumer, and putting their needs above his would be vital to his success. He understood that if you help enough people get what they want, you naturally get everything you want.

William knew that you can't buy success on credit, especially when the bank turned him down. He learned that you have to pay in full and upfront with a plan—with action and with discipline to see the plan through. So, with a few dollars in his pocket, a true friend as a business partner, a supportive family, and the willingness to take a chance to do something big, William started Universal Windows Direct—distinguished as one of the fastest-growing and most successful home improvement companies today! His simple philosophy of "treat the employee right, treat the customer right, and the company will do all right" has proven to be a formula for success!

His story and the principles in this book are applicable to anyone in a sales or leadership roll. Whether you are new to selling or leadership or are a thirty-year veteran, you will become motivated to do better and reach for more! You wont be able to help yourself from beginning your journey to what you can become. His ideas, passion, and integrity would benefit all that choose to listen to him.

You see, William, like most strong leaders, is egocentric, but he has struck a balance between ego and humility—something only few great leaders learn to do. When leaders find the way to do this they become magnets of influence, and people naturally want to be around them. Leading becomes easier because there is nothing fake about it. That wasn't always the case with him! Thank you for letting me punch you in the face! I hope you enjoy this book as much as I have and start to apply the ideas and principles William lays out so you can to get everything out of life you want!

Thank you, William,

Brian N. Smith

PREFACE

There is nothing new in the world of selling! Yes, you read that correctly.

So why should you read this book? The answer is a simple one: The majority of rhetoric and selling techniques have not changed, however, what has changed is the consumer. We have less time than ever with a prospect to build value in our products and services. Over the last ten years the average attention span of a consumer has dropped from 12 minutes to just 8![1]

Most salespeople are culpable of wasting the prospect's time; at some point, we have all been guilty of "showing up and throwing up" on our prospects. We overload them with a lot of information, hoping to cross the magic threshold of "they heard what they needed" to make a buying decision. In some cases that tactic works. In others, it frustrates your prospects, leaving them with a bad taste in their mouth.

So what is at the root of this all-too-common approach that has given way to the negative connotation of being a salesperson? The simple fact is that the majority of sales professionals do not know the true psychology of How, Why, and When a prospect is comfortable making a buying decision. I have trained and consulted

---

Forbes. "Customer Behaviour Is Changing: Check Your Assumptions," last modified November 26, 2014,http://www.forbes.com/sites/adrianswinscoe/2014/11/26/customer-behaviour-is-changing-check-your-assumptions/

with thousands of sales professionals, and not one of them has ever been able to answer those questions. I compare that to being a brain surgeon and not knowing where the brain is located!

Through a great amount of self-education and dedication to the profession of selling, I have created a system that teaches the How, the Why, and the When a prospect makes a solid buying decision on their own accord. There is truth in the saying, "people love to buy, but they hate to be sold." Think of this body of work as CliffsNotes that can prepare you to become a more effective sales professional.

The best part is that if you commit to this material, you will create a selling scenario where everybody wins—most importantly, your prospects win. You will have fulfilled their wants, needs, and desires, and you will have done it in a timely manner.

ACKNOWLEDGMENTS

I have to thank my beautiful, supportive wife, Addy. She believed in me before anyone; she invested in Universal Windows Direct when the bank would not. I wouldn't be where I am today without the love of a good woman. Thank you for putting up with my long work hours, the constant travel, and my overinflated ego—you always bring me back down to Earth when needed. We live in beautiful Chagrin Falls, Ohio, and have the world's most spoiled cocker spaniel, Scout.

I also have to thank my business partner, Mike Strmac. We have been friends since the second grade and have been hustling together since we were kids. It is a luxury to have a business partner whom you can trust. Together, we can accomplish anything we set out to do. "Who's the big winner? MIKEY IS!" Thank you, Mikey.

Furthermore, I am grateful to my management team. They have bought into our vision and execute it on a daily basis. Without Chad Howman, Justin Kiswardy, Todd Maynard, Eric Sears, Chris Jarvis, Chris Dysert, Bob Sharkey, Steve Sevinsky, and Michelle Kerr, I would never have been able to pull off this project. Thank you for your hard work and dedication to Universal Windows Direct.

I have been blessed to have many great mentors in my life. I have to acknowledge the authors and sales trainers who have inspired me to take my career in sales not only seriously but to another level:

Zig Ziglar, Tom Hopkins, Brian Tracy, Dave Yoho, and Rick Grosso have all had a direct impact on shaping my destiny. I also have been inspired by Earl Nightingale and Anthony Robbins, who have taught me how to think properly.

ABOUT THE AUTHOR

At an early age William was different from other kids. He wasn't just interested in making money—he was addicted to the transaction side of selling. He loved the action, or as some would call it, the hustle. Growing up in his family's used car business, he sold his first car at the age of fifteen, and from then on, he was hooked on the process. At dinner when other fathers and sons would talk baseball stats, William and his dad would role-play selling situations from earlier in the day. William loved that every situation in the sales profession—win, lose, or draw—is a learning experience.

In high school, he was your classic C+ student who used personality to get to graduation. He then began bouncing around from college to college, finally ending up at The Ohio State University.

For beer money during college, he got a job going door to door setting leads for a home improvement company. He enjoyed it and eventually got promoted to canvass manager, where his job was to recruit, train, and maintain thirty-plus college students—a priceless experience he compares to herding cats. After graduation from a different university—the School of Hard Knocks—he went into sales, then into sales management. As a sales rep, he had such a high success rate that he was asked to teach other people how to sell; that is when he discovered his purpose and true passion in life—sales training. He realized the positive effect he could have on other people by teaching them more than just how to sell but also teaching them how to think. He learned that the more value he added to others, the more valuable he became.

Parlaying all of his experiences and taking a chance on his abilities, he cofounded Universal Windows Direct in 2002 with less than $3,000 in cash. Universal Windows Direct is now one of the largest home improvement companies in America and has locations from coast to coast.

The purpose of this book is not only to add value to your career as a sales professional but also to change the projection of your life.

INTRODUCTION

A PASSION FOR SELLING

When it comes to selling, most salespeople waste a lot of consumers' time because they do not have the right approach: They're not asking the right questions, or they do not have the right purpose. In short, they're not fulfilling the consumer's needs and wants.

Too many people get into selling because they're lazy and think that sales is going to be a way to basically make money fast. In truth, selling can be the lowest-paying, easiest job in the world, or it can be the highest-paying, most-demanding job in the world.

To achieve an above average existence, you need to take the time to commit to your craft, to learn by reading and studying. If you make this kind of commitment, then you will be transformed as both a sales professional and as a person because you will discover your purpose, a "why" for what you're doing.

When I first started in sales, I made a mistake that most rookie salespeople make: I was concerned about myself, my commission, and how much money I made. Really, it was all about *me*.

I didn't mature in my role until I went to different seminars and read the wisdom of thought leaders such as Zig Ziglar, Tom Hopkins, and Anthony Robbins. Through them, I learned that if I focused more on consumers' wants and needs and not on my own wants and needs, I would gain their trust in a timelier manner. The goal, to paraphrase Ziglar, is to help enough people get what they want, and then you will get what you want. By asking the right questions—not just making a string of statements in a row—you will keep the consumer engaged and will stay in control of the selling situation.

I'm sure you're familiar with the initial reaction of the consumer in a selling situation. The first things they say are, "No. I'm not interested," or "I'm just looking." Even if you get past that initial stage, they will say, "Just so you know, I'm not buying anything today." And the consumer has every right to say those things because early in the process, they don't know you, they don't know your product, and you haven't built any trust with them yet.

When you take a consultative approach to selling and when you're truly there to help the consumers, then you will earn their trust faster than the salesperson who is just there to reach into that person's wallet.

There is a myth that great sales people are born great communicators. The opposite is actually true: the best salespeople are developed and become great listeners. When you take the time to listen and employ some of the techniques I'm going to teach you in this book, you will "wow" your consumers and build their trust. They will see you as different than other sales reps because you are actually interested in their needs and wants instead of just trying to shove a product or service down their throats.

Think about it: When was the last time someone sincerely asked you what you wanted? I'm not talking about the server who took your lunch order yesterday, I'm talking about someone who was truly interested in discovering what you wanted out of a business relationship or a selling situation.

This is one of the situations we role-play in the program I teach: We practice not just asking the questions but how to ask the questions in the most sincere manner—and mean it—because you really want and need to know the answers. And in today's world of short attention spans, you must be a better-prepared salesperson; you must be ready to get to the point. When you do that, the consumer will appreciate you for not wasting their time.

There's really nothing new in selling (not to take away from my influences), but what has changed is the consumer—and our challenge as professionals is to figure out how we can make the sales process more impactful and more efficient because that's what will help you make a better living.

WHO AM I?

I was one of those C+ students who made it through high school using my personality and charm with teachers. When I went to college, I took classes, but I didn't really enjoy school.

One day, my roommate asked if I wanted to go on an interview with him. I was a sophomore in college and I needed beer money, so I went along for the ride. We ended up in a neighborhood where he handed me a clipboard and said, "We're going to knock on doors." Although I had started selling professionally in my family's car business at age 15, and I was used to earning people's money and loved the transactional side of the selling process, to say I was outside my comfort zone would be an understatement!

I ultimately went along and, when I knocked on that first door, I almost lost my lunch. Despite my fear, I did knock, and I got my first lead. Today, I look back and I think, "What if I hadn't knocked on that first door?" Where would I be today? What would I be doing?" I am grateful for the lesson learned from noted thought leader Anthony Robbins, you must learn to be comfortable in uncomfortable situations, because fear is paralyzing.

After that, my job was basically to generate sales calls for the company's salespeople. I enjoyed it so much that I ended up managing a division of college kids: My job was to recruit, train, and maintain the team. The company had an approach that worked, and it was the first time I was exposed to a formal sales process.

About two years later, two of the members of the company decided to leave The Ohio State University area and start their own home improvement company, and they invited me to join them. In truth, I had been struggling to complete my degree, so I returned home to Cleveland to join them in the venture. They started their business out of a bedroom in a house, and I was promised—through sweat equity—ownership at a future point in time.

So I started selling for that company and soon I moved into management, where I discovered my true purpose, which was sales training. I had been so successful at selling that I was asked to train the other reps. Out of a desire to be a better trainer, I attended several seminars and digested any positive reading material I could get my hands on. This helped me to develop the selling and training systems that we teach today in my company.

Although that company really took off, through miscommunication and the fact that we were literally kids, I was ultimately denied the ownership opportunity that I was promised. Consequently, I began to grow unhappy with my job. At the time, I was dating my future wife, Addy, and she urged me to begin my own company. However, I was letting fear hold me back because, although I knew how to generate leads and get sales, I knew nothing about the manufacturing or installation pieces of the business.

Then two things happened that ultimately helped me take a leap of faith.

One day I came to the office and the owners were having a big laugh. When I asked them what was so funny, they told me that the previous evening one of our sales reps had "crushed an old lady" by arranging purchase of the company's products through a third mortgage. "She'll be gone before those windows are paid off," they roared. The fact that they thought it was hilarious made my stomach turn; I was in complete disagreement with the ethics of the company. I didn't like how the owners treated their customers, and I didn't like how they treated their employees.

Still, I struggled because I was a 25-year-old sales manager making great money, driving a new car, and living in a condo with a private balcony overlooking Lake Erie. Once again, I was stymied by my fear of the unknown; I was happy with my life, but very unhappy with the means by which I obtained it.

The second life-changing event happened as I was driving to work on a clear, blue-sky, early September day. I was listening to shock-jock Howard Stern on the radio, and I thought he was doing a bit about New York City being under attack—sort of an Orson Welles "War of the Worlds" kind of radio show. But I pretty quickly realized that the streets of downtown Cleveland were vacant.

When I got to the office, there was only one car in the parking lot. As I walked in the door, I saw the owner's face and heard a U.S. military fighter jet flying over. At that point, I knew the radio broadcast was no fake. It was September 11, 2001.

I got back in my car and headed for home, and on that ten-minute drive, I realized that life was short, and no matter what I was going to do with the rest of it, I wasn't going to do it for that company any longer.

A FATEFUL LUNCH

Left: Mike Strmac, Universal Windows Direct, Cofounder and CFO Right: William Barr, Univeral Windows Direct, Cofounder and CEO Photo: Benjamin Margalit, Margalit Studio

Also working at that start-up was my best friend since second grade, Mike Strmac. Mike started as a canvasser and eventually went into sales. He wasn't happy either and he had the same entrepreneurial spirit as I did. So one afternoon, we went to lunch at the Clifton Diner in Lakewood, Ohio to discuss our future. We discussed starting all kinds of different types of business models. Home improvements made sense to us, but guided by one basic principle: We were going to treat people like people. We were going to be fair and make clients happy, and we were going to have a company culture where people enjoyed coming to work.

We decided to start our own company, so we submitted a written business plan to the Small Business Administration, but we were turned down for a small business loan. I'll never forget us sitting in the parking lot of Key Bank in Cleveland, Ohio—we were devastated. Anthony Robbins says, "It's in your moments of decision that your destiny is shaped." We had a decision to make—go groveling back to where we weren't happy or gamble on ourselves. So the decision was made—with only $3,000 in start-up capital, we went to work.

Our first office was a 300-square-foot space over Al's Pawn Shop, which was across the street from a methadone clinic. We began selling our windows door-to-door, wading through the snow-covered streets of Cleveland, Ohio.

Today, we are the tenth-largest company in our category in North America. We managed to thrive through the Great Recession, and today our stores and dealerships are in more than forty cities. We've changed innumerable lives by employing countless people, and we'll do north of $70 million in sales this year.

I feel very blessed to be where I am today, and I marvel at the fact that it all began because I overcame my fear of the unknown and knocked on that first door.

Since then, I've perfected a selling system that's really geared toward today's consumer. I know that the most precious resource anyone has is time, and I know the How, Why, and When people buy.

After hearing sales trainer Tom Hopkins talk about the five reasons a consumer will or will not buy, I combined my knowledge and experience with what I had learned to design a selling system that covers those five reasons. My system recognizes that the best way to cover a consumer's objections is to go through a process that leaves them with no choice but to buy from you because you've removed all the barriers.

One of my mentors, noted sales tactician Rick Grosso, impressed in me the old adage of how to get to Carnegie Hall through "practice, practice, practice." Becoming a great sales professional takes practice, and unfortunately, in the beginning, we're all stuck practicing on our prospects. That can be an expensive learning curve. But that's the beautiful thing about selling; there is something to learn in every situation.

If you're in sales, then you should have a passion and drive for it; every time you make a sale, you should get a feeling in the pit of your stomach. If you don't get that feeling, Wal-Mart is hiring greeters. If you have the passion, it's not even work. That is why it's the greatest profession in the world.

CHAPTER 1

FIND YOUR PURPOSE

S uccessful selling starts with honesty and integrity.

As a young sales representative, I didn't understand that. I didn't realize that it is not possible to achieve real success as what I call a "taker," a salesperson who only has his or her own interests in mind.

Most salespeople have that kind of mentality; they are really out for themselves, and that's what has given the sales profession a bad rap. As I mentioned, some salespeople are guilty of just "showing up and throwing up," spewing out a bunch of information that doesn't mean a thing to the consumer. They just provide a lot of facts and features hoping they cross a "magic threshold" where the consumer has heard enough of what they needed to hear to make a buying decision.

But if you are a salesperson who has integrity and you have the consumer's wants, needs, and desires in mind, then you are going to be not only more effective but also more successful.

I learned this the hard way. At a young age, while working at my family's automobile dealership, I sold my neighbor a car and then made the mistake of celebrating how much commission I had made on the sale. My words got back to my neighbor and upset her, so as you can imagine, she wasn't in a big hurry to refer me to any of her family or friends.

That's just one of the hard lessons I learned in the selling profession—it's not about how much you make; it's about whether or not you made a difference. That comes from having the right purpose in mind, which is "what is best for the consumer?" Did the consumer need those extra add-ons? Or did you just throw those on because you were instructed to do so to make a bigger commission? There's a fine line between being successful and taking advantage of a consumer.

As a sales professional, you must realize that consumers are putting their trust in you. They are coming to you for help because you are the expert in your field, and they are going to take your word, for all intents and purposes, because dealing with your product is what you do on a daily basis. It's no different than when you meet with an attorney or an accountant. You're taking them at their word because that's their expertise.

DON'T BE A HACK

One of the reasons for my success is that I truly don't care about money. Until you can let go of your focus on money, you are not going to be hyper-successful. In the end, we are not going to be measured by how much stuff we had or how many properties we owned or how many trips we took. We are going to be measured by the impact we have on others. I saw that firsthand with my father. He was not a rich man, monetarily, but he led a rich life. He passed away earlier this year unexpectedly, and at his memorial service, an unbelievable number of people came out of the woodwork to pay their respects. This didn't necessarily surprise me, but it gave me a comforting feeling knowing that he had had such a positive influence on so many people. Groups of former employees gathered around and shared stories of lessons they'd learned from him. People revered him for teaching them how to "put food on the table." Others talked about his legendary "come to Jesus" talk—a pep talk that helped several people get back on track and reminded them why they were blessed to be in sales. Witnessing this reinforced my purpose. I realized that, if I stayed the course, I could also have a positive impact on peoples' lives.

Even though I had grown up in the family business and learned selling from an early age, my father did not want me to become a salesperson, because of the feast-or-famine nature of the business.

When I first left college and came home to work with some former associates in their new home improvement business, I lived in my father's basement. My hardworking, middle-class salesman father had wanted me to be an investment banker, but after six years in college, it just wasn't happening.

I will never forget his disappointment when I told him I was going to sell windows for a living. But the next morning at the breakfast table, after what I'm sure was a restless night for him, he sat me down and made me promise that I would not be "a hack." He made me promise to really commit to self-development, to learn from all the great mentors on the subject, and to take the selling profession very seriously. That is the same advice I am sharing with you.

If you are going to be a serious salesperson, then you must live and breathe sales. You must read all the books, listen to the tapes, and attend the seminars. By making the commitment to develop yourself as a professional, you are separating yourself from the crowd. Then, when you get into a sales situation, the consumer won't know exactly why you're better than the last salesperson they dealt with—they'll just get a better feeling because you will be a more polished, well-read student of the game.

WHAT IT MEANS TO BE A "GIVER"

One of my mentors, Zig Ziglar, says that if you help enough people get what they want, then you will get what you want.

When we first opened Universal Windows Direct, everyday on my route to work, I drove by the offices of Big Brothers, Big Sisters of Akron, Ohio, and there was a sign on the door that read: "Eighty-nine kids waiting to be matched." I drove by that sign for almost a year, and the number never changed.

So one day, I decided to drop in, and I ended up volunteering to be a Big Brother. I remember thinking that I had extra time because I owned my own company, and business was starting to pick up, so why not give back?

They matched me up with a little brother named Patrick, a six year old whose father had died when he was only a couple of months old. Patrick and I did everything together, from going on fishing trips to attending Cleveland Browns football games and Cleveland Indians baseball games. Through being Patrick's Big Brother, I discovered something very interesting—the more I gave to him, the more I seemed to get back in gratification.

During that time, I also started training groups of salespeople. We had begun our dealer program at Universal Windows Direct, and we were bringing in people from across the country. That's when I realized that the best way to give back was to mentor people who needed to be taught a skill.

That giving turned into consciously helping others after a life-altering event at a seminar I went to by Dave Yoho, another one of my early influencers. I entered the room thinking I was a pretty accomplished individual, until one of his associates, Brian Smith, asked me: "William, if I told you that I was going to punch you in the face, but after I punched you in the face you would make twice as much money—would you let me punch you in the face?"

I told him, "Sure, punch away."

He replied, "You're good at what you do, but until you drop your ego and you start helping others, you're done growing professionally and personally."

I went to dinner that night with a table of my peers, but they all had companies that were worth five or ten times more than mine. That was a motivating punch in the face to me. That is when I rededicated myself to the trade of continuous learning and growing.

So while I started out as a selfish salesperson, over time my attitude evolved into one where I knew I could make a difference in people's lives. That, combined with the culture of Universal Windows Direct from the start—which is to create a working environment where people want to be—has brought us to where we are today.

There is a wealth of knowledge out there if someone wants to become a professional salesperson and self-educate. The amount of energy and effort you put into learning your craft will determine your success. Your level of success is in direct proportion to the amount of energy you expend.

The system I've put together comes from a lot of self-educating, either from reading and attending seminars and learning from the leaders in this business or from first-hand experience. It comes from being in thousands of homes from coast to coast, working trade-shows in hundreds of different cities, and basically getting "punched in the face," so to speak.

Chapter 1 Takeaways:

- Successful selling starts with honesty and integrity.

- It's not about how much you make; it's about whether or not you made a difference.

- Take the selling profession seriously and commit to self-development.

Make It Personal:

- What drives your passion for selling?

- What life events have influenced your purpose for selling?

- What opportunities can you take advantage of to continue learning and developing as a salesperson?

- What can you do today to help someone get what they want/need?

CHAPTER 2

ADOPT A POSITIVE MENTAL ATTITUDE

A positive mental attitude is a daily diet that is paramount to success in sales (and in life).

Setting and maintaining a positive attitude will determine your outcome on not only a daily basis but also affect what you achieve throughout your lifetime. Understand that you can control what kind of a day you are going to have within the first few minutes of waking up. As an example, imagine this is how your day starts: You wake up late because your power went out and your alarm never went off, so you're late to work. You look outside and see it is a cold, rainy, miserable day. We have all been guilty of deciding right then and there that it is going to be a long, crappy day. The amazing thing is, in my experience, my days are self-fulfilling prophecies. This example day goes exactly as you called it. You're late for work, so you proceed to get behind an elderly driver going under the speed limit. Just for good measure you hit every red light on your way. You finally get there, and you left your presentation at home! The day is shot. I believe that this day was lost right from the second you made the decision it was going to be a long, crappy day. From that negative attitude all these events were set into motion, and you got the exact morning you asked for. The good news is if you understand this type of thinking you can reset your attitude and finish the day on a positive note. I have had several days where I have had to set or even reset my attitude before I started my day.

It all starts with making a good decision on a daily basis that you will have a positive mental attitude. What it boils down to is a simple concept: what you focus on, good or bad, you will achieve.

THINK ABOUT, THANK ABOUT, BRING ABOUT

Starting with a positive mental attitude involves the conversations we have with ourselves every day; salespeople especially go through this—they ask themselves if they're in the right place at the right time and if they're doing the right thing.

The problem with most people's internal dialogue is that they are asking themselves the wrong questions. In my experience, most people I come across are negative; they were either raised in a negative environment, or they just find it's easier to go through life being gloomy—misery loves company, right?

It doesn't help that we live in a society with a twenty-four-hour negative news cycle. In a typical, hour-long news broadcast, whether it's local or national news, 95 percent of the content is negative. If I look back over my forty years on Earth, mankind should have been destroyed innumerable times, whether by AIDS, the Avian flu, Y2K, the Mayan calendar, the Ebola Virus or what have you. That is what we're inundated with on a daily basis. Why? Because pessimism sells; people buy into it because it is easier to be negative.

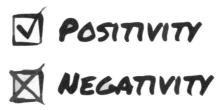

Even if you are a religious person and you attend an hour-long Sunday service each week where you get a dose of good news from a spiritual leader, it is still difficult to stay positive all week when you are balancing that one hour against a 24/7 dose of negative news.

It's no wonder that when someone takes so much garbage in, garbage tends to come out—it is easy for our daily intake to basically determine our daily output.

There's also a trap that we can fall into, which is allowing others to put labels on us. For example, in America we use standardized testing in schools. But what if when a kid has to take one of those standardized tests he's just having a bad day? Then he is likely to get slapped with a "learning disabled" label just because he scored poorly on an aptitude test. In his early years, some of the most important people in his life are those educators—and now he has authority figures telling him that he has a problem learning. At that moment in time, not only is an excuse born, but a path is set. He has been put in a box and told he's a certain way and that there is a path he's supposed to follow. What he does not know yet, unfortunately, is that the world is run by C+ students.

Now let's look at his twin brother who was having a good day when he took the same aptitude test. He scores so high that they tell him he is gifted. He gets better books, he's put in classes with smarter students, and he has access to better technology. He is being told by the same authority figures that he's talented and smart. Here again, the outcome is written, and he will likely follow the path of the label he has been given.

But it does not have to be that way.

Here is a simple exercise to help you understand what I'm saying: Start by thinking of the happiest day of your life, the day you experienced complete bliss. Maybe it's the day you met your spouse (a big one for me), the day you got married, or the day your child was born. A blissful day for me was when my partner and I won the Ernst & Young Entrepreneur of the Year award. When we were up on the stage high-fiving each other, I had an absolute feeling of accomplishment and bliss as I thanked my wife and colleagues.

Stop for a moment and think of the happiest experience of your life. (Really, do this now to get the full effect.) Note your posture. Are you standing or sitting up straighter and taller? How do you feel at this very moment? Chances are you feel great, you feel positive, and your body language conveys that.

Now, clear your mind and let's start over.

This time, I want you to think of the saddest, worst day of your life. Maybe it's the day you were fired or when you or someone you know was diagnosed with an illness. For me, it was when I was a fourteen-year-old kid and my Mother passed away unexpectedly. It was absolutely the worst day of my life because there was so much uncertainty and fear. I can go back in that moment right now and actually feel the sadness of that day. Now stop reading, close your eyes, and take yourself back to the saddest day of your life. If I were to look at my own posture in the mirror, I would no longer be smiling, and my head would be down. How do you feel? Chances are you're overwhelmed with negative feelings, and your body conveys that.

What can you learn from this experiment? What can you learn from thinking very happy and then very sad thoughts? You can begin to understand that *being negative or positive is a choice that affects us mentally and physically.* Thankfully, we get to determine which emotions we let in.

Now let's do one last exercise: I want you to try to be both positive and negative at the same exact time. Try to be both happy and sad. (Go ahead... see if you can do it.) It's impossible, isn't it? If you cannot be both positive and negative at the same time, and you're the one who gets to decide which side of that fence you sit on, why would you choose to be miserable on a daily basis? After doing this exercise and realizing that I get to choose which emotion I let in, I have decided to be positive on a daily basis. As a salesperson, your daily outlook on life is going to determine how much success you have.

> BEING NEGATIVE OR POSITIVE IS A CHOICE THAT AFFECTS US MENTALLY AND PHYSICALLY.

Instead of garbage in, garbage out, why not choose positive influences? Listen to positive, motivating ideas as you drive to work. Read motivational literature. Surround yourself with people who are also positive thinkers.

Henry Ford said, "Whether you think you can, or you think you can't—you're right." He understood that whatever you decided you wanted to do, good or bad, you were going to have that outcome. Needless to say, Ford knew a thing or two about building a successful business and breaking out of a label.

Attitude is up to you. Your mind is a fertile field of soil, and whatever you plant in that soil you're going to harvest. Through positive thinking, Universal Windows Direct has gone from a 300-square-foot office to one of the biggest companies in our category. Every year for the last fourteen years, we have achieved every single retail goal that we set for ourselves, and even through the great recession of 2008-2009, Universal Windows Direct experienced year over year growth. And if you look at our situation, the odds were stacked against us—my business partner barely finished high school, I was kicked out of college, and we had only a few thousand dollars to start with.

The second piece of a positive mindset is to focus on the things you are thankful for; when we verbalize what we're grateful for, we continue to attract more of those things. I am very thankful for my ability to communicate and my ability to help others think in a different way that helps them be successful.

President William Jefferson Clinton, whether you love him or hate him, was a perfect example of vision achieved. He grew up poor, but when he was four years old, he verbalized that he wanted to be president of the United States. When someone at the age of four says they want to be president, you have a tendency to laugh them off. But we all know how that turned out.

When Jim Carrey went to Hollywood, he was a struggling standup comedian. He knew one day he would make it, so he wrote himself a $10 million check and carried it with him always. He gave himself five years to reach that goal, and at nearly the five-year point, he realized that he had indeed achieved it because he was getting paid $10 million for the movie *Dumb and Dumber*.

Likewise, I had a personal experience of my own. One of our written goals in our ten-year plan is to have two hundred locations across the United States. We track our locations on a wall map of the United States; we use red pushpins to indicate our current locations, green pins for our target market areas, and yellow pins for someone we're negotiating with.

One day I decided that if we were going to grow, we needed more pins, and one of the locations I pinned that day was Springfield, Massachusetts. There was no particular reason for my choice—we didn't have any connection to the city—I just remember thinking we needed a dealer there. About a week later, my office manager asked me if I wanted to take a call—"He says he's heard of you," she told me. I originally told her to route it to my voicemail because I was busy at the time. But before she could, I asked her, "Wait. Where's the call from?" When she told me Springfield, I remembered the pushpin, so I took the call.

I ended up going to the city on a speaking engagement, and after the first training session, he became a Universal Windows Direct dealer.

So again, whatever you think about and are thankful for, you bring about. It is all about what you focus on—good or bad, positive or negative.

RESPECT YOURSELF, YOUR PROFESSION, YOUR PROSPECTS

It is very important that, as sales professionals, you hold yourself and your profession in the highest regard. Selling is the greatest profession in the world; you can make more money in sales than in nearly any other profession. Because you don't need any preconceived formal education to be a great salesperson, it's one of those professions where, if you are well-read and you practice your craft, your income is virtually unlimited.

One of my early mentors Rick Grosso taught me that, when you're green, you're growing; when you're ripe, you rot. So when you get to that point in life when you think you know everything, you stop growing professionally and personally, and you are basically stuck in a rut. Earlier I talked about how Brian Smith, one of the top earners in this industry, "punched me in the face" by telling me, "You're good. But you're not as good as you think you are." Until that time, I had been in a rut. I was doing well, but I was just cruising through my career. At that moment, I experienced a paradigm shift in the way I was thinking. What he told me was an eye opener; getting punched in the face was a good thing.

After that conference, I was motivated. I began developing a new technique that helped our monthly sales numbers double inside of ninety days. My personal income didn't double, but my company's did. I remember thinking, "Wow, I am so glad that I got punched in the face."

Besides having a positive attitude toward yourself, you must also have a positive mental attitude toward your company and your products.

During the sixties and seventies, Xerox and IBM were world renowned for their training programs. People would take less money to go work for Xerox because they knew the experience of learning how to execute the company's selling system was worth foregoing the income for what they could go on to accomplish later.

Regardless of your profession, we are all actually in sales. Teachers must sell the idea of learning to students. Organization leaders must get workers to buy into the company's mission statement. Politicians try to sell the public on their agenda. If you are selling a product or service right now, ask yourself, "Am I completely bought in? Do I own what I sell?"

Selling is the transference of feeling and belief. The level of feeling and belief that you have about yourself and your product will be transferred to the consumer. Conversely, consumers don't want to buy from people who don't believe in what they are selling. As I learned from Bob Hiner, the national sales trainer for Associated Materials Incorporated, in a selling situation, your prospect buys you first, your company second, and your product and services last. So you must buy into the way the company you are working for does things. Your job is to execute the company's business plan with passion, feeling, and belief and then transfer that to consumers so that they tap into your emotion—so that they actually buy in.

People buy emotionally, and they justify it logically. It is your job, as a sales professional, to create an environment that is so strong toward your product that the consumer cannot do anything but believe in what you're selling. They need to feel good and feel justified

SELLING IS THE TRANSFERENCE OF FEELING AND BELIEF.

about their purchase. The goal is to create an environment where the details, such as price or money, become secondary.

Your attitude also counts when it comes to your prospects. For starters, as a sales rep, you should never be above generating your own leads. In our industry, we refer to someone who is dependent upon company leads as a "lead baby." But your company is only going to generate so many opportunities for you. The most successful salespeople are those who understand that their attitude toward lead generation will determine their income. You should always have the mindset that you are never too good to go fish for yourself.

Most importantly, you must treat everyone with respect; do not prejudge them in any way. All salespeople, including myself, have been guilty of prequalifying based on age, looks, or preconceived notions of a credit situation. I know I'm on the receiving end of this sometimes because when I go shopping I tend to dress like a homeless person: camouflage shorts and a ball cap (my wife laughs at me). In fact, sometimes I'll dress down for the sole purpose of seeing how the sales rep is going to treat me. If he ignores me or acts like I should not be shopping at his BMW dealership, then I know he is not the salesperson I want to deal with.

THE MIRROR EXERCISE

So how do you change what you are doing today? First, recognize that it takes twenty-one days to form a new habit. Here is a daily ritual that I used to become a more positive person. I call it "The Mirror Exercise." It centers on asking yourself the right set of questions to get your day started.

The way "The Mirror Exercise" works is this: In the morning, when you're looking at yourself in the mirror as you're getting ready for your day, start asking yourself a set of questions. Here are the ones I ask myself, along with some of my answers:

- **What do I have to be thankful for?** I'm thankful for my wife Addy, my dog Scout, and my ability to communicate in a clear manner.

- **What am I grateful for?** I'm grateful for Universal Windows Direct and all the committed people that I have at the office who work hard even when I'm not present. I'm also grateful for being in the greatest country in the world, where opportunity is everywhere if I just look for it.

- **What am I proud of?** I admit, the process of writing a book scared me tremendously, but I'm proud to have finally undertaken the task. The first time I landed a large speaking engagement of four hundred people, I was petrified and almost didn't walk on stage. But I overcame that fear, so I'm proud of that. As I said earlier, in order to break out of the status quo, you must get comfortable with being uncomfortable.

- **Who loves me?** My wife loves me, my friends and family love me, and my dog loves me.

- **Who do I love?** My wife, my friends and family, and my dog.

When you focus on what you have, not on what you don't have, you will experience a shift in your thinking after only three weeks. It can be something as simple as, "I'm grateful I have a roof over my head," or, "I had a good meal last night." Everyone has something to be grateful for. The key is this: whatever you are thinking about and focused on—positive or negative—that is what you will bring more of into your existence.

Life is 10 percent of what happens to you and 90 percent how you respond to it. The easy way to respond to a crisis is to go into a hole; the difficult way is to go through the crisis and learn from it.

The billionaire businessman Richard Branson says that, if you look at any crisis long enough, you can turn it into an opportunity. When you learn to turn disadvantages into advantages, then doing so just becomes a part of who you are. The processes I'm teaching you will help you get through rough patches and begin to evolve until you don't need to practice anymore; an upbeat attitude just becomes part of who you are. You will become that positive person who people want to be around.

One of the challenges of becoming a positive person is that your coworkers, friends, and maybe even your family—people who haven't been trained to think in this manner—will not understand why your world is always "sunny and 75." But that's okay; To make an omelet, sometimes you have to scramble some eggs. With that said, in order to remain positive, you may have to change your social circle, including some of your family members. If you want to be positive, you have to surround yourself with like-minded people.

Let me share a couple of stories with you about the power of positive thinking.

Five years ago, my Aunt Emy, who is also my Godmother, was diagnosed with stage 4 uterine cancer. At the time, she was living a very busy lifestyle. Once she was diagnosed, instead of watching her focus on the cancer, I watched her make a very conscious decision to live and to cut out any negativity in her life. With her family's support, she decided to have fun and spend time with her grandkids and have huge family parties that she had no business throwing as she was going through three rounds of chemotherapy.

She changed her daily diet of what she allowed in, and because of this, she is still with us, fighting to this day! She never lets the cancer get her down or define her. That proved to me that if you have the right attitude - if you cut out negativity and focus on the positive— then you can really go up against just about anything.

Your attitude will also help put things in proper context.

Back when we had only one location, I had a conversation with my father in which I told him I was going to open two hundred locations of Universal Windows Direct. He thought I was crazy. So I asked him, "Well, how many people live in the United States?" He guessed, and then I told him, "Out of those three hundred and twenty two million people, don't you think that I can get 199 people to believe in me?" Putting it in that context, to me, made it sound pretty easy. I liked my odds. And that attitude has really helped shape who we are and where Universal Windows Direct is today.

Chapter 2 Takeaways:

3 Ingredients for a Positive Mental Attitude:

- Think about.

- Thank about.

- Bring about.

Make It Personal:

- What do you think about most often?

- How are your thoughts affecting your attitude?

- How is your attitude affecting your success?

- What will you do today to improve your attitude?

CHAPTER 3

SET GOALS AND TAKE ACTION

Setting a goal is easy; achieving that goal is often another matter. But I am going to share with you a four-step process to help you develop the skills needed to understand the different types of goals and how to achieve the goals you set.

Most people really do not have defined goals. When I do my training seminars and I ask a roomful of people how many of them have a goal, I typically get a showing of three or four hands.

Next I ask: Is that goal verbal or written? Of those three or four, typically only one has a written goal.

Then I ask: "When you go grocery shopping, how many of you—or your spouses—make a list?" When I ask this question, half of the people in the room raise their hands.

> THE DEFINITION OF SUCCESS IS A WORTHWHILE WRITTEN GOAL WITH AN EXECUTABLE PLAN OF ACTION WITH PRECISE DATES THAT YOU ARE PRESENTLY MOVING TOWARD.

Now think about this: half of the people make a grocery shopping list so they don't double-up on peanut butter, but they have not taken the time to make a list for their life's destiny.

For a lot of people, that is a real "punch in the face." It's a real eye-opener to be in a professional-improvement classroom and have no defined direction in life.

Now, it is common for people to approach goal setting as what I call "The New Year's Resolutionist." Those are the people who, on January 1, go on a diet, join a gym, plan to lose ten pounds, and so on. How long do those goals last? On average, they last fewer than two weeks. Even if those goals are in writing, they often end up at the bottom of a birdcage, and we all know what happens there.

So goal-setting is about having a defined, written goal. And that begins with understanding the definition of success.

As I have come to know it, the definition of success is a worthwhile written goal with an executable plan of action with precise dates that you are presently moving toward.

The beautiful thing about this definition is that the moment you decide that you want to be successful at something and you put your plan on paper, you're already there because you have begun the process.

I have defined four steps to setting and achieving goals:

STEP ONE:
ABSOLUTE CLARITY

The first step in goal-setting is to get absolute clarity—make a decision on what you want. Until you decide what that is, you're what I call a "wandering generality"—you really have no purpose.

How do you decide what you want? I like to tell people to become childlike. When we were kids, we all wanted to be astronauts and rock stars; how did we end up becoming accountants and lawyers? It's okay to be a little bit ridiculous when you're deciding what you want because nothing happens until you make that decision.

Now, how do you get clarity? Many people get their best ideas in the shower because it's one of the few places they can be for fifteen to twenty minutes without distractions—no cellphone, no news cycle, no one chirping in their ear. I am sure someone has cured cancer in the shower and then they got out and their mobile device dinged, and that great idea disappeared because of the distraction.

Find a quiet place and take as much time as needed to meditate and ask yourself, "What do I want? What am I looking for? What am I trying to achieve?" Your answers may surprise you.

So the first step to effective goal setting is to get clarity. Again, do not be afraid to think big. Do not allow someone else to limit what you want to achieve. This is your dream, your goal. I know that the bigger I think, the bigger my result.

STEP TWO:
TAKE ACTION

The second step, when it comes to goal-setting, is to take action; you must put your plan in writing—this will always drive a result. Putting it in writing means you decide on (and record) exact dates, numbers, and other details, and you break it down to the simplest of tasks.

Start with the larger goal. Let's say my goal is that I am going to open two hundred Universal Windows Direct locations. Again, on the surface, that sounds like a lot of hard work, and it is. But, if I break that down and say, "Okay, I need to sell twenty of them a year over the next ten years, which means I need to sell 1.6 of them per month, every month, and to sell 1.6 of them I need to get in front of one hundred people a month." Now I know that every month I have to reach out to one hundred people. In this way, I am not focusing on the big plan, the two hundred total, but I am focusing on a smaller task that will help me reach the next result. That makes my goal digestible and much more attainable.

Sales is about numbers: You undoubtedly have a quota, and you know your average ticket, and you know how many prospects you must see and how many of those must convert to sales. If you do not know your numbers, then I suggest you spend the time to figure them out. To develop a tremendous goal of selling $100 million worth of windows, you must know what you have to do on a daily basis to make that happen.

One reason we have been successful at Universal Windows Direct is because we set yearly, quarterly, weekly, and daily goals, and we have one-year, five-year, ten-year, and one-hundred-year brand plans. Without that kind of planning, I cannot guarantee that the company is going to be here as a brand a century from now.

Again, step two is to take action: put your plan in writing and create a blueprint for yourself. The more detailed the plan, the better.

STEP THREE: VISUALIZATION

Step three is visualizing your goal in the present tense. This is where the money is made.

People are guilty of remote-control goal-setting; when you drop the television remote control under the couch and then go to retrieve it, you take a swipe and miss, making it go a little further out of reach. This happens with goal-setting when people use poor word choice. For example, a typical goal might be, "Someday, I would like to have $1 million." Well, the problem with "someday" is that it does not show up on any calendars—none that I have seen anyway.

The words we choose set our destiny. For example, some motivational speakers say, "act as if," which to me means it has already happened.

Instead, visualize in the present tense; close your eyes and engage your senses. This makes it real in your mind's eye—in that split second, your brain does not know the difference.

For instance, let's say I have a goal that I want to have my own private jet. When I close my eyes, I see myself exiting the jet and walking down the ramp. My coworkers are with me. It's a sunny day. I can smell the jet fuel and hear the engine running. My company's logo is on the tail and I can see the tail number. In that split second, I am there.

The most powerful word in the English language is "imagine"; with imagination, anything is possible. Walt Disney passed away before he finished the Magic Kingdom, and when a reporter said to Walt's brother, "What a shame Walt wasn't here to see this finished," Walt's brother laughed and told him, "If Walt hadn't seen this in his mind, do you think we'd be standing here in the happiest place on Earth?"

When you're imagining, really let your mind soar. You cannot be afraid to think something outrageous. If you do, you're holding yourself back.

One of my early influences, Anthony Robbins, also talks about creating an "anchor," sometimes known as a "power move." An anchor, or power move, is a physical association with a victory or an achievement. Anchors are stimuli that call forth states of mind and their associated thoughts and emotions. For example, Tiger

Woods had his fist pump and Michael Jordan had the tongue wag. Some salesmen pound the top of the car roof when they make a sale. When you create that association, every time you go to do your power move—your fist pump, finger snap, or whatever the move— no matter what is happening at that moment, you're taking yourself back to that victory, to that time when you felt like you accomplished a goal or achievement.

For instance, every time I snap my fingers, I take myself back to the moment I sold our first dealership. The buyer had just agreed to the sale. As I was walking to the counter to pay for lunch an overwhelming feeling of excitement and accomplishment washed over me. I felt like I was floating on air! Out of excitement, I snapped my fingers and created an anchor. That anchor has served me well. Every time I snap my fingers, I can go back to that victory. My anchors and power moves helped me go onstage that first time I was about to speak in front of four hundred business owners.

Anchors are like goals; both are magnets to get you through those times when you're asking yourself, "What am I doing?" They help you remind yourself, "I have a purpose. I have a 'why,' I have something I'm working toward."

STEP FOUR:
THE ASSOCIATION OR THE FEELING

Now you have made a decision, put an action plan in writing, and visualized it in the present tense. Imagine in your mind's eye you have achieved what you set out to achieve!

How does that feel? Do you feel a sense of accomplishment and pride? Invincibility and freedom? Euphoria over the possibilities? By identifying and capturing your feelings at the moment of visualization, you will discover your purpose. This is step four of goal-setting: it's about the reason you set out to accomplish your goal, the purpose for whatever it is you have decided to achieve. The best part is that you do not have to worry about the "how"; you just need faith and purpose.

Most people set a goal and they make the mistake of basing it around monetary terms. If you take a look at money, it's really nothing but a stack of green paper. But people are obsessed with it. What do you need green paper for? It's not the money that you seek. It's the result that the money brings you, whether it's security or freedom or absence of worry. It's the "why": Why did you set out to accomplish that goal?

For instance, I have in writing, "My purpose is to write a sales book that will not only add value but will also change people's course for the better." Imagine how it's going to feel when someone tells me that they read this book and it changed their outlook.

If you go through these four goal-setting steps, instead of being one of those "wandering generalities" that I mentioned earlier—someone who has never taken the time to discover their purpose—you will reach that point where a feeling will wash over you and you will discover why you're doing what you're doing. This is a powerful feeling, but when you learn this process and practice it, you will find that anything is possible.

HOW TO BE ACCOUNTABLE

There are several types of goals. First is the verbal goal: that is the wish. Then there is the written goal with a plan; that is going to be more effective. But where the rubber meets the road is when you share your written and planned goal with others, whether it's with your family, your friends, your business associates or employees, or the general public.

In business, we share our five-year and ten-year goal with our employees so that we're all on the same page, and I am accountable to them to accomplish the things that I promise.

As a sales rep, if you tell others your plan, you are writing a contract with yourself and The Universe. And since you do not want to be known as a liar, you are essentially holding yourself accountable. For instance, if I tell my best friend: "My goal is to write a book and here's why," but then I don't get it done, then the next time he asks me about it I have to tell him, "Well, I didn't get it done." That is a driving force to make sure I stay on task.

If you share your ideas and then someone tells you your goal is too lofty or it cannot be done, then you will know you're on the right track; that is how I know I have a great idea. By sharing your goal with others it increases the odds of you accomplishing that goal.

Finally, you need to establish a daily ritual to keep that goal close. Start each day by thinking of your goal and how you're going to achieve it in a calm, cheerful manner, and then have faith that it will happen. Revisit your goal throughout the day and then again right before you go to sleep at night.

Very simply, I base the method for setting and achieving goals on the Sermon on the Mount: "Ask, and it shall be given you; seek, and ye shall find; knock, and it shall be opened unto you."

Now, I challenge you to use these steps to formulate a goal.

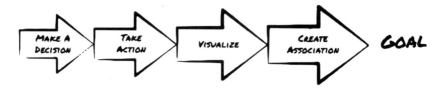

Now that you are in the right mindset, we are ready to break down the selling process. I always share one of my goals with new sales-people and dealers: "I can teach you how to sell; that's easy. My goal is to teach you how to think; that's powerful."

Chapter 3 Takeaways:

The Four Steps to Setting and Achieving Goals:

- **Step One: Absolute Clarity**. Make a decision as to what you really want to accomplish.

- **Step Two: Action.** Write your goal down and give it a timeline.

- **Step Three: Visualization (in the Present Tense).** Imagine that the goal has already been achieved, and create an anchor to remind you of that sense of accomplishment.

- **Step Four: Association (or Feeling).** Identify your feelings at the moment of visualization, and discover your purpose.

- **Final Note: Share your goal with anyone who will listen.** Your desire to follow through on what you said you would do will help you hold yourself accountable.

Make It Personal:

- What do you want to achieve most?

- Why do you want to achieve it?

- What does life look and feel like once you achieve your goal?

CHAPTER 4

UNDERSTAND WHY, HOW, AND WHEN PROSPECTS BUY

People in general really love to buy things, and Americans are conditioned at a young age to be consumers. When we're in kindergarten or first grade, we're led off to the Scholastic Book Fair to buy a book or two. By second or third grade, we're walking door-to-door and asking neighbors to buy candy or wrapping paper as part of a fundraiser. And even though, as I said earlier, everyone sells, the majority of professional salespeople do not truly understand the psychology of Why, How, and When consumers buy.

The truth is, people love to buy, but they hate to be sold. Consumers want to feel that they have arrived at their buying decision on their own accord.

Many organizations across America give their salespeople canned presentations, which are good presentations, but they do not teach anyone about why they work. As a trainer and educator, I have found that if someone understands the psychology of what they're doing, if they understand why a sales process works, then they are more likely to understand their purpose. As a sales professional, if you understand the love-to-buy, hate-to-be-sold mindset, you will be able to add a lot of value to a prospect's experience.

If I were to ask the top sales producer in any sales organization in America the five psychological reasons Why a consumer will or will not buy—I am talking real estate, financial brokers, lending institutions, home improvements, jewelry stores, automobile businesses—the majority of them may get one or two reasons right. But they really do not understand the basis of Why, How, and When people buy. As I said before, I liken that to being a brain surgeon and not knowing where the brain is.

I have put together what I call the sales CliffsNotes to help you because it's a career game-changer when you know Why, How, and When people buy. In this book, you will learn about the buying cycle and how every consumer has a different threshold that they need to cross in order to feel comfortable making buying decisions. For example, I may have to ask consumer A for their business three times while consumer B may buy immediately. Consumer C will never buy, regardless of what I offer.

> THE TRUTH IS, PEOPLE LOVE TO BUY, BUT THEY HATE TO BE SOLD.

You will also learn about being a prepared salesperson, because consumers love to invest with salespeople who have their act together.

Let me start by summarizing the five reasons Why a consumer will or will not buy. Regardless of the product or service, these five psychological reasons are universal; they are what make everyone tick.

1. Trust: Trust is the most important thing in selling.

2. Time: It's harder to get the attention of today's ultra-busy consumer. Our most precious resource is time; in the end, no one is going to wish they had more houses, but they are going to wish they had more time—I guarantee that. So it's vital, when you're dealing with your prospect, to get to the point.

3. Need/Want/Hope: People do not buy what they need; they buy what they want. If they do not want your products, they are not going to buy them. I will talk about how to create the need and sharpen the want, and then get the consumer into what I call the "hope zone." This involves "price conditioning," which is about dealing with your consumer's "want level" which is elevated when they reach a point in the process where they think the product or service may be priced beyond their reach.

4. Value: If I try to get you to pay $5 for a water bottle, and you think it's only worth $2, then you're not going to buy it because you think it's not a good deal. I will give you some great techniques for controlling the perception of value.

5. Urgency: You must give the consumer a true reason to take action today because consumers need some type of inducement to buy. We are going to cover how to

create that urgency and how to give the consumer a good perceived value. Creating a sense of urgency is one of the most underutilized tools for salespeople in a selling situation.

THINK LIKE A CONSUMER

For now, I would like you to step out of your sales professional shoes and think like your consumer. I am going to take you through five scenarios in which one of the reasons I just mentioned is missing so that you can see the likelihood of the sale happening. Often, consumers are not conscious of the reason—they just have a feeling that something is not right, so they will not give you the sale.

Remember, we're working on five different things: trust, time, need/want, perception of value, and urgency. And these work with virtually any product or service.

- **Scenario #1: Lack of trust.** Let's say I sell water softeners and come into your home and spend three hours with you, so you have invested a tremendous amount of time with me. You really need my product because where you live the water is not good. I am asking $10,000 for the product. You feel it's worth $12,000 or $13,000, so I have controlled your perception of value. Then I give you some type of inducement by saying, "Listen, I know you thought it was going to be $13,000. I'm only asking $10,000. If we can get this done today, we will do it for $8,000." In this scenario, four of the five things are qualified—time, need/want, perception of value, and urgency. But what is missing is trust. Maybe during my presentation I said something to you that did not quite sit right or did not meet your values. Well, if you do not trust me or like me, I could have the world's greatest product and value proposition, but you are not going to buy from me because people do not buy from people they do not like. That is why trust is one of the most important reasons why a consumer will or will not buy.

- **Scenario #2: Lack of time investment.** Let's say I come into your home and you already know who I am and you trust and love me. You need and want my product. The only hitch is that you can only give me fifteen minutes of your time due to a prior engagement. I am asking $18,000 for my product. I then give you a reason to take action today. You only feel (due to the lack of time I had to build value) it's worth $12,000. Besides the fact that you perceive it's overpriced, what consumer is capable of making an $18,000 decision in fifteen minutes? I know I can't.

- **Scenario #3: Lack of need/want.** Now I come into your home. You know me and my company, so you trust and love me. You spend three hours with me. I control the perception of value by asking $10,000 when you think the product is worth $13,000. And I give you a reason to take action today with a discount. The only problem is that you're looking at my product and you really do not need or want it. Let's look at the basic tenet here: Say you had your heart set on buying a red car, but after going through my process, you realize the model you want is only available in white. I could be the world's greatest guy, I could have the world's best value, and you could spend five days with me, but if the product does not come in red, you are not going to make a big investment or purchase because it does not fit your want or need.

- **Scenario #4: Perception of value.** Now let's say you come to the office where I sell my products— insurance—and you are thinking about investing with me. You already trust me because a neighbor of yours uses me. You spend three hours with me. You have a family and three kids and you absolutely need an insurance policy. I give you a reason to take action today with some type of urgency call or incentive. The only problem is, I am asking $10,000 for my products, and you feel they're only worth $5,000. So your perceived value of my product or service is half of what I am asking. In this scenario, you're not going to buy, because you do not want to overpay.

- **Scenario #5: No sense of urgency.** Now I come into your home. You trust and love me. I spend three hours with you. You need and want the product or service I am offering. I am asking $10,000, and you think it's worth $13,000, so you feel my product or service has value. But I do not give you a reason or inducement to take action today.

By now, I think you can probably tell that when I go into a home I do a pretty exciting presentation; I deliver with a lot of passion. But in all the years I have been doing this, I have never had a consumer at the end of my presentation throw their wallet on the table and say, "Go ahead and take it." I have always had to ask for the sale and to give the consumer a reason to take action. If I do not give them a reason, then they will procrastinate with a familiar phrase: "This all looks great, but I'm going to get back to you."

When the consumer and I are going through this process, it's the most important thing in the world to that consumer. I am the immediate; I am what is on their mind right then. But the minute I leave without that sale, I lose all control—the dog gets sick, there is a rumor of layoffs at the mill, or they get an unexpected bill. So what was a priority today is no longer important. We know from experience that if we do not earn their business the first time we see the consumer, the likelihood of earning their business altogether goes down drastically.

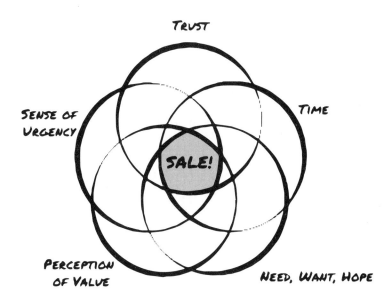

As I have just summarized, if just one of the five reasons for Why a consumer will or won't buy is missing, the likelihood of making a sale plummets.

But if you understand the psychology of Why, How, and When people buy, whatever product or service you sell, you will leave your consumer feeling good about buying from you. In fact, without a reason to deny you the sale, they will almost feel obligated to do business with you.

Remember, people love to buy, and they hate to be sold, and selling is about fulfilling their needs and wants—it's not about you; it's about them. Your job is to help them get what they want, and you want them to feel good at the end of this process.

When you know these five reasons Why the consumer will or will not buy, you can actually ask yourself throughout the process which component you're missing. Or, if you do not make the sale, then you can run through the scenario after the fact to understand which of the five reasons was missing. In this way, you can learn from every situation.

If you're a sales manager, you can also use these five reasons as a resource to replay what may have been missing when your reps do not sell.

With this process, you will learn to be the one bringing up the objections because, typically, the person asking the questions in the selling situation is the person who is in control. So instead of being a reactive salesperson, someone who is always responding to curveballs the consumer throws at you, you can be a proactive salesperson who actually brings up all the consumer's concerns and issues first and then covers them throughout the process. When you're a proactive salesperson, you're controlling the conversation.

In other words, which would you rather be: a thermometer or a thermostat? A thermometer takes the temperature, a thermostat sets the temperature. In a selling situation, would you rather be the one taking the temperature or setting it?

THE CHALLENGE

The challenge for you, as a sales professional, is to figure out how this system fits your product or service. How can you take whatever product or service you sell and design a presentation that will cover all five of these reasons and leave the prospect with really no choice in the end but to invest in that product or service?

If you're an average salesperson, this will make you great. In fact, if you're the first person in your company to figure this out, it will make you a star. If you're already a great salesperson, you will likely end up in management because people will want to learn why you're coming out of your selling situations with better results than anyone else.

In the end, the ultimate goal for any salesperson is to create brand advocates— consumers who love your product or service so much that they will tell others positive things about it. How do you do that? You make sure the consumer leaves the process feeling good, whether you sell them or you don't.

Again, if you understand these concepts, you will become a much more prepared and powerful salesperson.

In the following chapters, I'll give you techniques for mastering the five factors that determine whether your consumer will or will not buy. You must never move from one of these five factors to the next until you get a commitment, otherwise, you're wasting time.

Chapter 4 Takeaways:

The Five Reasons Why A Consumer Will or Won't Buy:

- Trust

- Time

- Need/Want/Hope

- Perception of Value

- Urgency

Make It Personal:

- What prevents you from buying something?

- Which of the five scenarios described in this chapter do you encounter most often?

- In what ways can you train yourself to think more like a consumer?

CHAPTER 5

BUILD TRUST

The number-one reason why someone will or will not buy is trust. If the consumer does not like you and if they do not feel comfortable with you, they are not going to buy from you, even if you have the world's greatest product or service—even if it's free.

I have two examples to prove my theory.

The first example is Zig Ziglar's, who said that a person standing on 42nd Street and Broadway in New York City wouldn't be able to give away ten free $100 bills in a row; someone is bound to refuse the $100 because they will think there is a catch involved. That unknown will shut a consumer down.

The other example is from my own selling experience. Universal Windows Direct, my company, works trade shows. In fact, we are a sponsor of one of the largest trade shows in America; our name is on the marquee. At the entry door of this trade show, we pass out a free bag; it's a nice bag that people can use to hold the literature they collect at this show. For us, of course, it's nice when, over a week's time, seventy thousand people are seen walking around with our company's name in their hands. But believe it or not, people turn us down when we try to give them a free bag.

For instance, I remember asking one woman if she would like a bag, and she turned me down. Right off the bat, she said, "I don't trust you. There's got to be a catch." So I asked her again, "Ma'am, are you sure? You're going to collect a lot of brochures. You're going to need a bag." Nope, she turned me down again. Finally, I said, "Well, you can always put your coat in it so you don't have to pay the coat check girl $1 to hold your coat." Then she took it.

In this scenario, I had to ask the person three times if she would like a free bag. If I have to ask someone three times if I can give them something for free, how many times do I need to ask if I am trying to get them to invest $15,000, $20,000, or $30,000 with me? How much trust is involved in earning their business at a high price tag when they won't even take a free bag?"

In a selling scenario, a consumer buys in a particular order: They buy you first, your company second, and your product third. Most salespeople understand this backward. They think it's all about the product and what the product does for the consumer. To a point, they are correct. But in reality, people want to buy from people they like and they connect with.

So how do you develop this trust? The best way to do it is to take a consultative approach. Consumers are typically very timid. They have their own expertise—they are a teacher or an accountant—but in a sales situation, they stay quiet and do not ask questions for fear of looking stupid. So your job as a salesperson is to make them feel comfortable and get them to open up by using your expertise to answer their questions; uncover their needs, wants, and desires; and find a product that fits in their budget. Then, if you cannot help them, show them someone who can.

> A CONSUMER BUYS IN A PARTICULAR ORDER: THEY BUY YOU FIRST, YOUR COMPANY SECOND, AND YOUR PRODUCT THIRD.

A typical conversation might be something like: "Today, my job as a professional is to educate you on what's available in the market and if I don't have a product or service that fits your needs, wants, and budget, then I'm going to tell you who to call." When you take that consultative approach and you become a problem-solver instead of a salesperson, then you disarm the consumer, which allows them to open up to you. They see you as someone who is not just trying to sell them something. I have had consumers actually admit that they did not know anything about the product and then thank me for taking the time to educate them on what was available in the marketplace. When you give them information, they see that you are the expert, and they feel comfortable making a decision.

Regardless of what you're selling, if you get to the end of your presentation and the consumer does not feel like they have enough information, they are simply going to tell you that they will get back to you, in which case they are not buying from you.

> WHEN YOU BECOME A PROBLEM-SOLVER INSTEAD OF A SALESPERSON, THEN YOU DISARM THE CONSUMER, WHICH ALLOWS THEM TO OPEN UP TO YOU.

So how can you set yourself apart from the crowd?

For starters, show the consumer that you truly care about their needs and wants by conducting a needs assessment in which you ask questions and then listen to the answers. There is a great myth in selling that if somebody is a great talker, they are a natural-born salesperson. Great talkers are not great salespeople; great listeners are great salespeople. Listening is the number-one way to develop trust in a selling situation. And it's a skill that must be developed.

Think about the society we live in right now—I call it our "selfie-centered society"—where everyone only cares about "themselves." No one listens to others, they just think about their own daily life. When was the last time somebody sat down and asked you what you really wanted or what is important to you? Does your spouse listen to you? Does your boss listen to you? Do your friends listen to you? In any restaurant today, you will see a couple dining together, but they're on their cellphones; they're not even communicating with each other. It's even depicted on television: in *The Sopranos* drama, the high-powered mob boss went to a professional therapist once a week because she was someone who would actually listen to him. By being someone who actually listens to the consumer, you will begin to build their trust and set yourself apart from their usual daily interactions.

THE THREAD TECHNIQUE

As a salesperson, if you develop your listening skills, you're going to uncover not only why you are in this selling situation but also what makes that consumer tick. The way we do this is through what is called the Thread Technique, which is a way of weaving the consumer's responses back through the conversation.

> GREAT TALKERS ARE NOT GREAT SALESPEOPLE; GREAT LISTENERS ARE GREAT SALESPEOPLE.

The technique begins by sincerely asking the consumer why they are considering purchasing your product or service or why they entered into the sales process in the first place. We use questions such as: "What do you want to gain? What are you hoping to get out of this process?" If you ask sincerely and you truly do care about the consumer, then something pretty interesting is going to happen. One, you will completely disarm the consumer because you will be the first person in a long time to ask them what they want. Two, you're going to begin to develop trust. And three, you're going to start the sales process.

After you ask the questions, then just shut up and listen. God gave us two ears and one mouth. We are supposed to use them in that proportion, especially in selling. Let the consumer tell you what they want—that is far more powerful than you trying to sell the consumer on what it is they should want.

Next, at Universal Windows Direct, we use what we call our "Talking Pad," which is basically a notepad. The Talking Pad is your best friend—use it to write down whatever your consumer says.

So when you ask them, "[Customer's Name], as a visitor in your home, I'd like to know, by getting brand-new windows, what are you looking to gain? What's most important to you?" and they reply, "I want to improve the efficiency of my home with a maintenance-free product," then write that down. This will let your consumer know you're really listening and that you are taking what they say seriously.

Once you have written down the answer, repeat it. Be aware that, if the consumer acts a little bewildered, it's likely because nobody—especially a salesperson—has really asked them what they want for some time. But when you repeat the consumer's words back to them, something really beautiful happens—you begin to build trust.

If you're the consumer, I can give you ninety-nine reasons why you should buy my product or service. But if you have one reason, that one reason is more important than my ninety-nine—because it's your reason. It came from you. There is a difference between it coming from you and me planting it in you. Because it's your reason, it's the best reason.

So with the Thread Technique—asking questions, writing them down on your Talking Pad, and then repeating them back to the consumer—you are using active listening skills to build trust.

The next step of the Thread Technique is the tie-down. This is about getting a commitment from the consumer. The best way to explain this is through a typical dialogue that we at Universal Windows Direct might have with a consumer.

> Sales professional: "You called me out, and I'm just a visitor. Tell me, by getting brand new windows, what's most important to you? What do you want to gain from this experience?
>
> Consumer: "I want the new windows to reduce our energy costs, and I want to update the overall look of our home.
>
> Sales professional: "Okay. So, to clarify, the reason you want to replace your windows is because you'd like to save on energy costs and improve the look of your home. Is that correct?" (Write down these reasons on your Talking Pad.)
>
> Consumer: "Yes, that's correct."
>
> Sales professional: "That's a great reason to do this project, isn't it?"

Now, how is a consumer going to answer that? They are going to say, "Yeah, it is a great reason." Of course it's a great reason, because it's their reason, and they are not going to disagree with themselves.

So you have reinforced the reason why you're in the selling situation, and you have uncovered the real reason why they want to buy. You now know what is really making this consumer and this buying situation tick. That is powerful.

When we instituted the Thread Technique at Universal Windows Direct, our sales increased by 40 percent. In addition, our demonstration time dropped because our salespeople were focusing on the consumer's true needs and wants. Without using this technique, you're just guessing. But with this technique, you will discover what the consumer's hot buttons are—those are what you focus on. You will still touch on the other features and benefits of your product or service, but do not focus on them, because that may be a waste of time. Your goal is to match your product and service with the prospect's exact needs and wants. If they say they want energy-efficient, maintenance-free windows, then what a coincidence—you just happen to have that product. The consumer needs A, B, and C, and you just happen to have A, B, and C. Plus, you also have X, Y, and Z.

Without the Thread Technique, you could spend thirty minutes talking about something that is not important to the consumer; it's not only going to turn the consumer off, but it's also going to waste their precious time.

You can also use the Thread Technique to close. In this scenario, think of it as a qualifier. The consumer wanted A, B, and C, and you  showed him A, B, and C, so other than the money, there should be no reason why you cannot earn the consumer's business.

For example, let's say I want to buy a sports car. I want a pre-owned, silver convertible with fewer than twenty thousand miles on it; those are my qualifiers. The first BMW dealership I go to, I find a red convertible with thirty thousand miles on it. Now I have a choice as a consumer: I can compromise my value system or I can keep shopping. I decide to shop on. The next dealership has exactly what I want! A silver convertible with twelve thousand miles—that meets all of my qualifications. Therefore, my choices are to buy it or waste my time and the salesperson's time. In this scenario, if a consumer tells you, "The reason I want to buy your product is A, B, and C," and you hit all those qualifiers, if they do not buy from you, that leaves them in a bit of a precarious situation because they told you this was why they were going to buy, and now they are backtracking.

OTHER TECHNIQUES TO BUILD TRUST

There are a number of other basic techniques to develop trust. Here are some that we use:

- **Set the tone and pace for the consumer.** Your demeanor can help control a sales situation. As a sales rep, you want to go into a situation calm, cool, and collected. If you're nervous, the consumer will sense it, and you will have trouble building trust. If you're excited, the consumer is going to be excited; selling your product is the transference of feeling and belief. If you believe in yourself and your product, then that is going to transfer to the consumer, who will buy into that emotion. So think of it as a mirror. Whether you're on the phone or in an in-person selling situation, imagine yourself looking in the mirror and ask yourself, "Would I buy from me today?" Send a memo to your face reminding it to smile. If you're not happy and you're not feeling good about it, the consumer is not going to either.

- **Use the consumer's name.** The most beautiful sound in the world is someone's name. Gwen likes hearing "Gwen" when I am talking to her, and it feels good because it's all about Gwen. That is just human nature; it does not make a person self-centered.

  When you're in a selling situation, make sure that you are on a first-name basis. Ask the person permission to use his or her first name, especially if you are dealing with someone who is your senior. Also, the consumer should know your name, your company's name, and the product's name. If they do not know what they're buying and who they're buying from, they're not going to be comfortable. If you're not great at remembering names, use your Talking Pad to write down the person's name and use it often, so that it becomes well known to you. You want to be on a first-name basis with the consumer so that you are all comfortable and are all friends, not strangers or adversaries.

- **Wear your brand.** In addition to looking professional—even if your attire is business casual— you also want to be branded. Have your company name everywhere. Again, make sure the consumer knows who you are and for whom you work.

- **Respect the consumer's time.** This is a recurring theme in sales. If you have an eight o'clock appointment with the consumer, that really means 7:45. We train our people that if they're going to show up at eight o'clock, they need to call the consumer as a courtesy and let them know.

- **Put down the cellphone!** The rudest thing you can do when you're in a selling situation is take personal calls, texts, or check social media. Do not be distracted by something that you have going on. You are basically telling the consumer that you're just going through the motions and that something or someone else is more important. When you're in front of a consumer and you are uncovering their needs, there is nothing more important. So put down and silence that cellphone.

- **Don't talk negatively about competitors.** Talking about competitors in a negative manner during a sale is an easy crutch that lazy, sloppy salespeople use. They figure they will get the sale if they rip their competitor and point out all the reasons why the consumer shouldn't buy that competing product. In truth, that is a tremendous turnoff to a consumer. And any moment that you spend talking about your competitor is one less moment that you're building value in your company's products and services.

Worse still, in some cases, you might be talking about a competitor that the consumer was not even considering. Now the consumer has another product to research, especially since you are so concerned about that competitor. I have seen this with my company; consumers call us all the time and tell us they heard about us from our competitors during a sales pitch. You also do not want to talk about competitors, because everyone needs to earn a living, and in the end, most products in a category are really pretty similar. What most consumers want is to buy from someone they trust and like. Badmouthing a competitor can injure your credibility.

- **Never ask for the sale based on your needs.** Never tell a consumer the reason they need to buy is because you're going to hit a bonus or you're going to win a contest. "I need to feed my kids," or, "Baby needs new shoes," are not good reasons to ask a consumer to buy. It's a complete turnoff, and in most cases, it's not even believable. This, again, goes back to their needs, not yours.

- **Build common ground.** I like to call this "building rapport." Find something that you have in common with the consumer. But it has to be real; if you do not like eggs, do not talk about making omelets. If you see by the animal-head trophies on the wall that a consumer is a hunter, and you start having a conversation about hunting but you're not really a hunter, it will take about sixty seconds for that consumer to realize that you're full of it. And once you break that trust, the consumer will see you as someone just trying to tell them what they want to hear.

One way to build common ground is by asking about a consumer's other major purchases, from the perspective of looking to make a similar purchase of your own. Ask the consumer why they made the choice they did, and you're likely to learn a few things about how and why they buy. For example, if you ask them why they chose to buy an Apple laptop and they reply that they did a lot of research and all the consumer reports told them that it was the best value, then you will know that they're the kind of consumer that likes to research products and is looking for good value. If they tell you they got a screaming good deal on it, then you will know that they're more impulsive and more likely to be sold on a price inducement.

- **Be an expert in your field.** Of course you should know your product, but you should also know your company history, industry trends, and your competition. Even though I said earlier not to talk negatively about the competition, you must know who they are, what products they offer, and their strengths and weaknesses. If you're the expert and you know about everything in your industry, that is going to help the consumer trust you and feel good about the process.

  Another way to build trust in this area is to tell consumers why you are with the company you're working for. This lets consumers see your conviction about your company and its products. Communicate to them with passion and pride.

- **Use voice inflection.** This is about being in control of your faculties and being able to put emphasis on certain words, which can change the meaning. Being in control of your voice inflection is huge—slowing down your pace when you need to slow it down, getting excited when you need to be excited. Just avoid being monotone, or you will really bore the consumer and shut them down.

- **Ask questions.** If you make more than three statements in a row, you are going to lose 50 percent of your consumer's attention span. Instead, ask questions to engage the consumer, get answers, and essentially force them to participate. If you ask a question and the consumer does not answer, then they are not paying attention. You have lost them.

- **Use "if" and "when."** There is a right way and a wrong way to ask for a commitment from your prospect. To take pressure off, speak in "if and when" terms. Think about the different connotations of the following questions: "Mr. Prospect, after seeing my impressive system, is this what you want to invest in today?" Or, "Ms. Prospect, after seeing my impressive system, *if* and *when* you invest, is this the *type* of system in which you see yourself investing?" In the first scenario, I am asking for a strong commitment, and if the prospect does not feel he can justify the sale because he needs more information, I run the risk of him being turned off, or worse, him saying no. In scenario number two, I take the pressure off with the words "if" and "when." Think about it; where do "if" and "when" fall on the calendar? Today? Tomorrow? Maybe never. The word "type" is also used because it's very general, and it allows you to solicit an easy yes from your prospect. The second question gets you closer to the sale, while the first question might push you farther away.

- **Avoid polarizing topics.** Try to avoid discussions about politics and religion or any other polarizing topics, if you can. Most of those conversations don't go well, and there is nothing to gain by talking about subjects that may place you in an adversarial position with your consumer.

- **Tell your company's story.** Be sure to share how long your company has been in business, the groups and organizations it belongs to, and any charities or social causes it supports. The more your consumer knows about the good things your business does and has been recognized for, the more likely you are to foster a relationship of trust.

Once you have implemented these techniques, be sure to get a commitment. Do not be afraid to ask the consumer whether they are comfortable working with you and your company. If the answer is "no," then slow down and ask: "What haven't I covered?" or, "What do I have to do to make you feel comfortable with me, because your comfort is important to me?" Once you get a "yes," that they are comfortable with you, then they have basically given you the green light that they trust you.

Congratulations! That "yes" means you have overcome the main reason a consumer will or will not buy from you, which is trust. Now that you have this TRUST commitment you can move on to the next stage. I cannot stress enough the importance of getting this commitment because if you do not, there is no point in moving forward.

Chapter 5 Takeaways:

Techniques to Build Trust:

- Use the Thread Technique.
- Set the tone for the consumer.
- Use the consumer's name.
- Wear your brand.
- Respect the consumer's time.
- Put down the cellphone!
- Don't talk down your competitors.
- Never ask for the sale based on your needs.
- Build common ground.
- Be an expert in your field.
- Use voice inflection.
- Ask questions.
- Use "if" and "when."
- Avoid polarizing topics.
- Tell your company's story.

Make It Personal:

- What techniques are you currently using to build trust with your consumers?
- How well do your consumers trust you?
- What will you do during your next conversation with a consumer to earn their trust?

CHAPTER 6

RESPECT YOUR PROSPECTS' TIME

Another one of the five psychological reasons Why a consumer will or will not buy any product or service is time.

Just put yourself in the consumer's shoes for a minute: If you're a consumer and you're thinking about making a major purchase, are you capable of making a $15,000 decision inside of fifty minutes? Most of us are not. In fact, there is an old saying in sales: If your price is too high, then your story is too short. In other words, you didn't spend enough time building value in the product or service.

Our challenge as sales professionals is that a lot of times the consumer will approach a selling situation from an adversarial viewpoint; they will want to keep you at arm's length.

In fact, I can use myself as an example. I hate to shop. I buy the same pair of shoes from the same salesperson, Carl, at Nordstrom's every time I need a new pair. Now, the mall is the last place on Earth I want to spend my Saturday. But when I walk in and Carl sees me and asks how he can help me, I always tell him, "I'm just looking, Carl." Even though I know I am there to buy something, and I know what I want to buy, I keep Carl at arm's length for two reasons: one, I'm afraid if I talk to him long enough, he might sell me that second pair of shoes that he always tries to sell me; and two, I don't really want to spend too much time with him because then I'll feel obligated to buy more. This all goes back to that basic psychology that consumers love to buy, but they hate to be sold.

The easiest way for a consumer to keep from being sold something is to keep that salesperson in an adversarial position. As a consumer, if you commit time to that salesperson, there is a chance you are going to commit money to him.

Let me give you some other examples of the consumer taking an adversarial position. We have a huge car company where I live, Spitzer Auto Group. The company has been in business for more than 116 years. One of the company's advertising campaigns involves different consumers going to the dealership with a "game face"—the consumers have strapped to their faces head shots of themselves making determined, intimidating faces. At the dealership, the consumers walk up to the salesman with this game face strapped on and they say, "We want that car, at that price." Right off the bat, they're saying, "Listen.

I don't want to hear any of your nonsense. Don't try to sell me something. Don't waste my time." Spitzer responds with a business model of "no-haggle, upfront pricing." The company touts how it creates trust and saves you (the consumer) time.

I do the same thing when I go into a situation as a consumer. I always remind my wife, Addy, "Don't fall in love with this product or service too fast. We'll lose that position of power to negotiate." Again, I put on that game face.

In my business, we call the appointment with a consumer a "lead." Let's say one of our reps has a "lead" at nine o'clock in the morning. Well, at eight o'clock, his prospects—Mike and Amy—over their morning coffee decide to have a "sales meeting" of their own. The only problem is our rep isn't invited. Why? Because their number-one topic of discussion is how they are going to say no to this pesky salesman. Mike and Amy are getting on the same page so they can be a united front. They say to each other, "Let's just get the quote and we will decide later, agreed?" or, "No matter how good of an offer, let's sleep on it." All these objections are predetermined and ready for you, the sales rep, when you hit the door.

Again, this is human nature. It does not make the consumers bad people. It makes them smart consumers. They have a game plan. The second they meet you, the sales rep, they usually throw that game plan at you. Within thirty seconds of meeting you, they will say things like, "Just so you know, we're not buying today," "We're just looking," "We're in the information-gathering stage," "I felt bad for the appointment setter, so I figured I'd let you come on out," "This is a free consultation, right?" "I have a brother-in-law whose cousin has a friend whose neighbor also sells this product," or, "I'm not really sure I even need your product or service."

Why does the consumer do this? Besides keeping you at arm's length because they do not want to invest time with you, they are right. At that point in time, when they have just met you, they are not buying from you.

Why do they believe that? Simple. They do not know who you are, and there is no trust built in; with no trust, there is no way you can earn their business. They do not know what your product offering is, so they do not know if they need or want your product. They certainly haven't spent any time with you, because you have been there all of thirty seconds. They have no basis of value because you have not told them any costs yet, and you have not had the chance to prove to them what your product or service is worth.

Giving a consumer a price right away is equivalent to me asking you the following question, "Hey, would you like to buy the boat in my driveway? I'd like $50,000 for it." Is that a fair price? That is all the information I give you: the location and the price. Of course you're going to start asking questions like: What kind of boat is it? How old is it? How many hours are on the engine? You do not have enough information to make a decision.

At the beginning of a sales process, the consumer has no basis of fact, so of course he is going to keep you at arm's length. They are not going to give you a commitment because they have invested zero time with you, so they're not obligated to.

From a sales professional's point of view, the more time you spend with someone, the more value you can build. The more value you build in your product or service, the more money it's worth. And money really represents security to today's consumer.

Your average consumer earns a decent living—let's say $50,000 a year. In a two-income household, where the husband and wife each earn $50,000, how long does it take them to bring in $100,000? One year? In reality, it takes two years; it takes them 730 days (365 days each) to gross $100,000.

Now let's say you're selling a product or a service that is $10,000. That is your asking price. If you just step back and take a bird's-eye view, you're asking people in a two-to-four-hour time span to spend 10 percent of their gross income that takes two years to bring in. So that time you spend with them must be valuable.

Your job, then, is to justify your price by building value. That takes time. Most consumers are incapable of making a big decision on short notice; that is one reason people procrastinate. As a sales professional, your job is to help the consumer make the decision emotionally and then justify their decision logically.

TRAINED VERSUS UNTRAINED EAR

When untrained salespeople hear the consumer say, "I'm not buying today," or, "I'm just looking," they have the tendency to shortcut or shut down their procedure because they will pre-qualify their prospect. They think, "These people aren't that serious. I'm not really going to do my job here."

For example, if you're a car salesman and your job is to do a walk-around presentation and take the consumer on a certain style of test drive, if you do not feel the prospect is serious because they're giving you all that pre-sale resistance, then your tendency is to say, "These people aren't serious, so I'm not going to spend any time with them. I'm just going to give them a price." That is exactly what that consumer wanted in that scenario. In this scenario, who is in control, the salesperson or the consumer? The consumer is in control. And as I have said, whoever is in control in the selling situation is the one who is going to come out ahead.

With some sales reps, there is also the laziness factor. If my fourth sales call of the day meets me at the front door and gives me all kinds of reasons why they are not buying, and I am not feeling like selling right then, I get to say, "Well it wasn't a good lead anyway." I can justify my laziness based on the consumer because I have that untrained ear.

Another trap the untrained ear falls into is where the consumer says, "I'm buying today. I already know your company. My neighbor has your product. My brother-in-law works for one of your guys." They start telling you all these reasons why they're going to buy. In this scenario, you give a big sigh and think, "Thank goodness. These people already know who I am. They already know my pricing. All I have to do is go through the motions. I'll take my shortcuts." Then, at the end when you ask them to buy, they say, "This all looks good, but I need a little more information." They do not feel justified because you did not spend the same amount of time. You pre-qualified them based on what they said.

We have a saying that you have to treat customers like friends and friends like customers. The biggest trap for a sales rep when they're selling to someone they know is that they do not spend the time with them building the normal value propositions. This could be your brother-in-law or your best friend in the world, but if he looks at your product and says, "I don't get it. I don't understand why it's X amount of dollars," then you basically just shot yourself in the foot, even though you thought you were giving that person the deal of a lifetime.

There have been times when I have shortened my sales process when selling to friends and family members. As a result, they thought they did not get as good of a deal because I did not go through my process and procedure. This is a mistake often made by salespeople who assume that their customers understand the value of what they're buying. Regardless of who you're dealing with in a selling situation, you must go back to the equation that time equals value, value equals money, and money equals security.

On the other hand, a trained ear actually gets excited. What if I told you that the vast majority of consumers that told me that they were not going to buy from me at the beginning of selling situation ultimately did buy from me? It was the consumers that said they were going to buy from me that didn't.

> REGARDLESS OF WHO YOU'RE DEALING WITH IN A SELLING SITUATION, YOU MUST GO BACK TO THE EQUATION THAT TIME EQUALS VALUE, VALUE EQUALS MONEY, AND MONEY EQUALS SECURITY.

Remember, the consumer wants you to shortcut. If they do not have all the information, then they feel justified in not making a decision; they do not feel obligated.

But I believe an educated consumer is an empowered consumer, and an empowered consumer can make a good buying decision. To empower someone, you must spend time educating them on all the benefits and value of your product or service. You must avoid being lazy and taking a shortcut.

GETTING PERMISSION TO SPEND TIME

When you come into selling situations, you are trying to separate consumers from their hard-earned dollars. To do that, they have to feel justified that they trust you, they need and want your products, and they have spent enough time in the process to justify why they're actually buying today. As sales professionals, we must earn the right to spend time with the prospects.

Here are several techniques for gaining permission from a consumer to spend his or her precious time.

- **Acknowledge the consumer's time.** An important technique is to acknowledge how precious the consumer's time is. We usually say something like, "I know how precious your time is, so I'd like to get to the point of why my product is better."

- **Set a positive, upbeat tone.** A great way to get permission to spend time with consumers is to let them know at the onset that, yes, you're going to talk about a product or service, but you're going to have fun doing it.

- **Take a consultative approach.** Use the needs assessment I mentioned earlier as a way of building trust. It can also set the tone for your selling situation and place you in a consultative position. This is basically a survey that reveals the consumer's needs, wants, and budget. It's designed to save time because it helps you find out exactly what the consumer wants and what their future plans are. Conducting a needs assessment is a great way to get permission to spend time with the consumer.

- **Be prepared.** In a sales situation, you must be prepared to have comebacks for those inevitable, early objections. If the consumer says, "I don't have time for you today; I just want a price," remember my boat example. Is it fair to say, "I have a boat in my driveway, and I'm asking $50,000 for it"? The consumer cannot possibly make a decision on your product or service when he has no idea what is really involved and what differences there are in quality. That takes time.

- **Walk and chew gum at the same time.** Another good technique I call "learn how to walk and chew gum at the same time" is about multitasking in a selling scenario. Don't stop presenting to use your calculator or laptop. Keep talking and calculating at the same time. If you stop, the silence is a mood killer, and you can lose your momentum.

- **Be entertaining.** If you take yourself too seriously when you're involved in a sales situation, the consumer is going to sense that. They're also not going to want to spend time with someone who is grumpy. We have a saying at Universal Windows Direct that grumpy salespeople have skinny children; what that means is that nobody wants to commit time to someone if they feel like the process is not going to be fun or educational.

- **Set an agenda.** An agenda is a type of short introduction where you're basically telling your prospect, "This is how this process is going to go." Essentially, the way we do this is to say: "My job is to educate you so you have all the facts and figures. So first, I'm going to tell you about my company. Then, I'm going to show you how my product is an investment and how you will get a return on your investment. Lastly, I'm going to go over the different products available in the market place." By telling the consumer that you're going to educate them, rather than telling them they have to make a decision today, you will begin building trust. Once you tell the consumer you're going to do A, B, and C, then the key is to stick to the agenda. Don't go off on tangents that do not add value to the sales process; these waste valuable time.

When setting the agenda, get a commitment. This is an agreement from the consumer that they understand what the process is going to be and that they are going to give you their attention. When you get that commitment, you can check off time as one of the five reasons Why a consumer will or will not buy.

Once you get a consumer to commit to giving you their time, it really prevents them from getting away from you or stopping the sales process halfway through. Getting the commitment of time helps you stay in control and prevents the consumer from mentality or physically checking out prior to you finishing the sales process.

Chapter 6 Takeaways:

Getting Permission to Spend a Consumer's Time:

- Acknowledge the consumer's time.

- Set a positive, upbeat tone.

- Take a consultative approach.

- Be prepared.

- Walk and chew gum at the same time.

- Be entertaining.

- Set an agenda.

Make It Personal:

- What's your normal response when a consumer tells you they're "just looking" or "not ready to buy"?

- Are you spending the right amount of time educating your consumers about your product(s) and/or services?

- In what ways do you show respect for your consumers' time?

- How can you make the time you have with your consumer more engaging and worthwhile?

CHAPTER 7

TUNE IN TO PROSPECTS' NEEDS AND WANTS

The third reason Why a consumer will or will not buy any product or service is the presence of need, want, and hope. This is what I refer to as the "How" they buy. There are four keys to How they buy.

Remember, in America, people do not buy what they need; they buy what they want. As Americans, we learn to consume at a very early age; by the time we reach adulthood, we are referred to as hyper-consumers.

A great example of buying what we want over what we need is an automobile. Nobody needs to drive a Hummer that gets five miles to a gallon when a Prius offers ten times the efficiency. Why do people buy them? Because they want to.

Consumers often come to us with a need. Your job, as a sales professional, is to sharpen their want or desire for your product or service. When you sharpen consumers' wants, and they fall in love with your product or service, then it's easier for them to justify separating themselves from their hard-earned money. That is the key: to take the consumer from needing your product or service, to wanting it, to hoping that it's affordable. When they get to this last area, which I mentioned earlier as the "hope zone," they are so invested in your product that when they find out they can afford it, they're relieved. You don't have to be a wizard or the world's greatest closer to sell something to somebody if they're relieved that they can actually own it.

The psychology driving this idea is similar to that of the classic takeaway technique. We often observe this with children. For example, if there are two six-year-old kids in a room and one of them is playing Nintendo and the other kid comes over and takes the controller away, the first kid experiences a sense of loss, and his want level goes through the roof. It's the same with adults—the more they think they cannot have something, the more they want it.

There are four key things a consumer looks for when buying a product or service. The combination of these four things is what I refer to as the "How" consumers buy. The four things are: Differentiation and Exclusivity, Upper Level Benefits, Price Conditioning, and Trial Closes. First, I'll break down each one of these individually, and then I'll tie them back together.

DIFFERENTIATION AND EXCLUSIVITY

The first key to "How" consumers buy is to differentiate yourself, your company, and your product or service.

Start by differentiating yourself. You must be a positive force for change. This goes back to being prepared, not being a hack, and putting your prospect's needs above your own. Remember, the consumer buys you first (then your company, then your product).

So how can you differentiate yourself? For starters, you can be better prepared and more entertaining. You can take the approach that you're a problem-solver; you're there for the consumer's needs, and you communicate that it's not about you—it's about them. Believe it or not, if you take the time to listen to the consumer and put your cellphone away, you're already going to be different than most of the salespeople today who put themselves above the consumer. So develop your listening skills and use the Thread Technique where you sincerely ask the consumer what they want and use your Talking Pad to record what they say. Build trust with the consumer, and you will differentiate yourself from the pack.

You must also differentiate your company in the marketplace. What does your company do better or differently than other companies in your category? Is it community service? Is the company socially committed? If your company has a certain purpose or mission, then it's your job to communicate that to the consumer to prove that your company is different. If you have great culture at your company, make sure that the consumer knows that. Also make sure the consumer knows that you love working for the company.

Another differentiating factor is your product or service; you must have some type of exclusive product. Is the product a local economy product? Sometimes the exclusivity may be in name only—just a different label—unfortunately. But if you are fortunate enough to have a product that truly has some differences, then you have what is called "a Unique Selling Position" (USP).

A Unique Selling Position is something you have that your competitors do not; in some way, your product or service is better than others. If consumers fall in love with your product or service because of its differentiating factor, then they really have no choice but to buy from you. Your job is to communicate in a clear manner your USP and how that benefits the consumer.

A Unique Selling Position and an exclusive product line also eliminate the doubt factor. Human nature dictates that if a consumer thinks that they can get your product or service or one like it for less money, they are either going to wonder about that or they are going to try to find it. If you leave either of those questions in the mind of the consumer, you have created an opening for the consumer to walk away without purchasing from you. The confused mind says NO! When you create an exclusive product line and have a Unique Selling

Position, you eliminate the consumer's doubt or desire to continue shopping. So a USP is very important; in fact, "exclusive" may be the most important word in the sales presentation.

Just to give you a peek at how we do things at Universal Windows Direct, we use that word "exclusive" in excess of one hundred plus times during a sales presentation because we want to make sure we communicate to the consumer that they cannot get our products anywhere else. This is our exclusive product line. We actually call it the flea/sledgehammer approach. Why do you kill a flea with a sledgehammer? Because it leaves no room for error or doubt.

UPPER-LEVEL BENEFITS

The second key to "How" consumers buy is to tune them into WIIFM Radio. That stands for "What's In It For Me?" They want to know, "If I invest in your product, how will it benefit me? What will it do for me? How will it improve my life?"

Our job as sales professionals is to communicate to the consumer in a clear manner the features and benefits of a product or service. But at Universal Windows Direct, we like to take the ordinary and add a true Upper Level Benefit to it; we communicate to the consumer how our product is extraordinary.

Just talking about the features of a product is what I call "the throw up." When you tell the consumer the benefits of the product, you are then adding some value. But what your product or service does for the consumer in the end is what really matters to them; this is the Upper Level Benefit, and it's up to you to connect the dots for the consumer.

An Upper Level Benefit is a benefit that you cannot put a price tag on. Let me give you some examples.

MasterCard has a series of thirty-second television commercials that demonstrate the power of an Upper Level Benefit. An older one of these is about a father and son at a baseball game. The voiceover says:

> *Two tickets: $46.*
> *Two hot dogs, two popcorns, two sodas: $27.*
> *One autographed baseball: $50.*
> *Real conversation with your eleven-year-old son: Priceless*

What does MasterCard understand? Forget about the $123 you just spent getting to the game and eating one lousy hot dog. You just had something you cannot put a price tag on—time spent with your son. That is an Upper Level Benefit.

So what are some Upper Level Benefits that your product or service can do that you can't quantify with a monetary value? Number one is time. We cannot put a price tag on our time, and it is the most valuable resource we all have. Websites such as Travelocity are basically tools that do all the research about your vacation or business trip for you. What the site is selling is not so much travel bookings but more so the fact that if you use their site, you will save time.

Comfort is another Upper Level Benefit—none of us can put a price tag on our comfort. If you're stranded in the woods and you have $2 million in a duffle bag, and you know that in order to survive the night you must burn every single dollar in the bag, there are very few people who are not going to burn all the money; burning every dollar is the only thing that ensures comfort and self-preservation.

There are billion-dollar industries built on comfort as an Upper Level Benefit. Look at the mattress industry: What is "Sleep Number" really selling at the end of the day? It's not mattresses. They're selling comfort.

Safety and peace of mind are invaluable benefits, especially if you have loved ones. ADT, which is a huge security company, runs a TV ad that shows a mother and daughter in the backyard playing soccer. The mother and daughter enter the home, and the mother flips on the ADT security system in time to have it trigger when a creepy burglar breaks through a door and enters the home. ADT saves the day. If you're a parent or family provider and you see this commercial and you do not have an ADT home security system, you think to yourself, "I don't have what I need to secure the safety of my family and give myself peace of mind."

Security is another thing people cannot put a price tag on. That is why Americans invest in 401(k)s and life insurance. They're buying that security for the future. One of the greatest ad campaigns of all time came from Prudential, which advertised that buying Prudential insurance (an intangible thing) is buying a piece of the rock, something far more tangible and solid.

Freedom is another Upper Level Benefit; we cannot put a price tag on our freedom. When Jeep, a great American car company, sells a Wrangler, what it's really selling is freedom. It's selling the ability to go off road and not have to follow the rules.

Health is another Upper Level Benefit. People invest billions of dollars in their health, but nobody can truly put a price tag on health. If you take a look at Steve Jobs, founder of Apple, a true visionary, he would have given back all the money in the world to have more time and better health.

All of the big companies that I mentioned understand that what we sell is a product, but it's a byproduct of what we offer.

Your challenge as a sales professional is to take a look at your product and service and say, "Yeah, I sell a widget, but what does my widget really do?" Are you communicating to your prospects just a bunch of product features? If so, you're really missing the boat.

Remember, we're talking about differentiating yourself. If you're a sales rep who talks up all the Upper Level Benefits your product offers and your competitors are just giving features and basic benefits, you are going to look better. Your product is going to be worth more because it does more. For instance, if my competitors are talking about plastic and glass and I am talking about safety and security, whose product is going to be perceived as worth more?

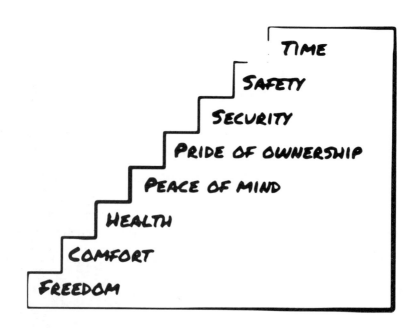

PRICE CONDITIONING

The third key to "How" consumers buy is price conditioning. This is about controlling the perception of value or money for a product or service.

As a sales professional, you must get comfortable with the idea that a good deal is a state of mind; if the consumer thinks it's a good deal, it is. The beautiful thing is that if you understand this as a sales rep, then you get to create that state of mind.

I'll use the example of two homes, A and B. Let's say I go into home A and sell windows to the homeowner, John, for $10,000, and he loves me and he thinks he got a great deal. Then I go next door to home B, and I sell the same number, style, sizes, etc., of windows to Joseph for $5,000, but he thinks he got ripped off and he despises me.

In this scenario, even though Joseph paid half as much as John, did he get ripped off? You likely think, no, he did not, since he only paid $5,000 when he should have paid $10,000. Did John get a good deal? Again, your intuition is likely telling you, no, he did not, because he paid double—he paid $10,000.

The answer actually is in reverse. It's counterintuitive. If John paid $10,000 and he thinks he got a great deal, then he did. If Joseph paid $5,000 for the same thing, and he thinks he got ripped off, then he did. It does not matter what I think. It does not matter what the public thinks. It only matters what Joseph and John think. A good deal truly is a state of mind.

Our job as sales professionals is to control the perception of value during the sales presentation. If you're great at controlling the perception of value, everyone is going to feel like they got a tremendous deal, which is important. You want to leave them with such a good feeling that they not only become customers, but they also become clients and eventually brand advocates. A brand advocate will shout your praises from the rooftops.

Price conditioning also eliminates sticker shock and lessens the consumer's need to shop around.

Let me share one of my own examples as a consumer.

A couple of summers back, Addy and I decided we wanted to have a third car, a convertible for the summer. We wanted to pay cash for it because we thought a monthly payment would lessen the fun of owning a convertible; it would just be another thing to worry about. So we set a pretty reasonable budget of $15,000 to $20,000, and we decided that if we couldn't get it for that price, we wouldn't buy it.

The first place we went to was a Jeep dealership because I had owned Jeeps when I was younger, but everything was $25,000 or more for a decent one.

Then Addy mentioned that she had seen some convertibles online at the BMW dealership. My grandfather retired from General Motors, and our family had never owed a foreign car, so I was hesitant.

But Addy can sell me on anything, so she convinced me to go and look at BMWs. There were three pre-owned Z4 convertibles on the lot; none of them had price stickers. Well, I fell in love with one right away, but with only fifteen thousand miles on it, I just knew it was a $40,000 vehicle. It actually upset me a little that I was so enamored with a vehicle that I knew was out of the range we had agreed on.

When the salesman told me the car was only $17,000, a calm washed over me. I had price conditioned myself that this was a $40,000 car. When I found out the dealer only wanted $17,000 for it, I was instantly relieved. We test drove it, and we loved it, so I called my dad who was still in the car business and I told him about it. He said, "That's only worth about $14,000." Suddenly, I was upset again because the car was overpriced. This emotional rollercoaster took place inside of thirty minutes.

So I told the sales rep I wouldn't give him more than $15,000, because it was in such good shape. We ended up haggling a little—something I enjoy doing—but we got the car.

In that scenario, I went from thinking the car was worth X amount of dollars and being upset, to being relieved, to being upset again because I realized it wasn't worth what they were asking, then to being happy because we settled on a price I felt was fair. That is what we mean by price conditioning or a good deal being a state of mind.

A different consumer could have thought that car was worth more money and paid more for it. But the only thing that matters in this deal is what I thought. What's funny is that even though I teach this stuff, I still get caught up emotionally because of price conditioning, and I don't even realize that it's happening to me until later.

Sales is the perception-is-reality business. Your product or service is worth only what your consumer perceives it's worth.

All companies price condition in some form or fashion. One of the most basic examples is Wal-Mart. When you go to Wal-Mart, items are priced, for example, *Was* $19.99, *Now* $16.99. They are showing you what I call a value spread, which is basically the difference between what you thought the product was going to cost and what it actually does. That difference between the "was" price and the "now" price is perceived value. The company knows that if it shows you what the product used to cost and what it now costs, then you feel like you got a deal, which gives you the permission to buy. Wal-Mart even posts the savings amount ($3 in this example)

because it doesn't want to gamble that the consumer will not do the math.

Another example is the way consumers love using Kelley Blue book when purchasing a used car. If Kelley Blue Book lists a car at a value of $21,000 and the consumer only pays $18,000, they feel they got a tremendous deal.

Infomercials do this, actually in a pretty funny way. They will say: "This product is $19.99. But wait, if you order now we're going to double your order." You need that extra mop, right? That is the perceived value of getting two for the price of one, and it's a form of price conditioning.

TRIAL CLOSING

The final key to "How" consumers buy is trial closing.

By definition, a trial close is getting a simple commitment along the way that the consumer wants what you have. If you go through an entire sales presentation, and the consumer never says yes to you, or they do not agree with you at least once, do not be shocked if they don't agree with you at the end of your sales presentation.

In a Universal Windows Direct presentation, we get between sixty and eighty trial close commitments; a consumer says yes sixty to eighty times. It's a lot harder for the consumer in the end to say no to me when they have been agreeing with me for the last hour and a half. These trial close commitments are very important.

Throughout the sales process, you're going to get little commitments and big commitments. An example of a big commitment is after you lay out the agenda and the consumer says, "Yes, I'll spend time with you." If you do not get that commitment, you cannot move on. We talked about the trust factor, asking the consumer, "After hearing about my company, if and when you do a project like this, is my company the type of company you feel comfortable investing with?" That is a big trial close commitment. After you do a masterful presentation and sharpen the consumer's want, ask for a commitment: "Does my product or service meet your needs? Is it the type of product or service you can see yourself investing in?" When you ask that question and the consumer gives you a yes, then you have their commitment.

It's amazing how some salespeople never even ask for a commitment at the end of a sales process.

Another nice thing about trial close commitments is that they help you stay in control. You're asking questions, and remember, whoever is asking questions is in control. Trial close commitments are great questions to ask to ensure you're not making three or four statements in a row and losing your consumer's attention.

TYING IT ALL TOGETHER

So how do we tie all four "Hows" (Exclusivity, Upper Level Benefits/WIIFM, Price Conditioning, and Trial Closes) together into a selling scenario? If you can take your product and plug in those four things, you're going to be a more effective, more profitable salesperson, and you will be able to help other people in your company sell more.

Here is a short vignette to show you how we do this at Universal Windows Direct using products we sell every day.

One of the advantages of choosing my exclusive UniShield technology is we have a unique product called Super Spacer. Super Spacer is a structural foam developed by NASA. It's how we seal our glass.

The reason I share that with you is all of our big box, big brand competitors who charge thousands of dollars for a window use some form of metal. Have you ever seen a window that has fog in between the glass? This seal failure is due to condensation caused by the metal spacers. With our exclusive UniShield, we have a product that outperforms in testing. It makes your home more comfortable. You can't put a price tag on your comfort. Can you?

We also have a health smart tag. It's physically impossible for mold or allergens to grow, so it makes your home healthier.

Then we give a lifetime warranty that if the glass ever sweats or condensates, we replace it for free. Wouldn't you prefer the peace of mind that this is the last window you're investing in? How upset would you be if you invested $1,000 in a window that eventually failed?

I have to ask, after taking a look at the differences in what's available on the market today, putting price aside, which one of these would you love to see performing in your home? I'm sure you'll agree, my exclusive UNI-Shield is a superior product, isn't it?

Here are some of the techniques I used in this vignette:

- I used the word "exclusive" several times.

- I told you about my Unique Selling Position of Super Spacer versus metal.

- I told you about the Upper Level Benefits of my product—what's in it for you is comfort, health, and peace of mind.

- I price conditioned because I prepped you that the other companies were going to charge you $1,000 for a product that was inferior, whether it was in performance, warranty, or both.

- I asked for several trial close commitments from you confirming that you understood how my product was better.

In this scenario, I hit all four qualifiers of "How" a consumer will buy a product. I was different. I told the consumer what the product was going to do for them. I price conditioned them. I got a commitment.

If you understand and execute these four keys to "How" consumers buy, you will have given a masterful presentation. This masterful presentation is designed to not only create the need, but sharpen the consumer's want for your product or service. In an ideal selling situation, the consumer starts to wonder if and hope that your product or service is within their budget. Once they enter this "Hope Zone" their want level goes through the roof. In fact, they will be relieved upon realizing that it's actually affordable.

So again, your challenge is to take your product and figure out, "How do I highlight the features of my product and hit all four qualifiers, making it priceless?"

Chapter 7 Takeaways:

The Four Key Things (the "How") a Consumer Looks for When Buying a Product or Service:

1. Exclusivity and Differentiation

2. Upper Level Benefits / WIIFM

3. Price conditioning

4. Trial closings

Make It Personal:

- How are you, your company, and your product different and better?

- What does your product do for the consumer beyond features and benefits? Hint: Consider Upper Level Benefits, time, safety, security, pride of ownership, peace of mind, health, comfort, and freedom.

- How do you control the perception of value?

- How do you secure simple commitments throughout the sales process?

CHAPTER 8

BUILD VALUE THROUGH COMMUNICATION

M ost people think that money makes the world go 'round. In all reality, it's the perception of money.

This is the fourth reason a consumer will or will not buy any product or service—the Perception of Value or Money.

When you hear a consumer saying, "That sounds like a lot of money," or, "That's too much money," as an objection for not purchasing your product or service today, what they're really saying to you is, "In my opinion, the value proposition of your product or service is too low."

As a salesperson, you must realize that your product is only as good as it's perceived, and it's up to you to master the science of price conditioning. Your product or service must be worth more than you're asking, otherwise it does not look like a good deal.

Just take a look at society as a whole, and look at some of the perceptions of brand or perceptions of value. For example, if you go to a factory that produces Polo shirts, they're producing two lines of shirts at any given time. These shirts are identical; they have the same cut, the same color, and the same collar. The only difference is one of them has a little Polo emblem on the left chest and the other one does not.

When a consumer goes to a Polo store on Madison Avenue or 5th Avenue in New York City, they are going to spend $120 for that shirt. They feel justified because they are buying a brand that they identify as valuable. They are saying, "I wear Polo."

But that same shirt without the logo is available at a discount retailer for $15 to $30. It has the same cut and the same color, and the only thing missing is the logo. Another consumer will pay $80 for the shirt with the Polo logo at an outlet store; he will feel like he got a real deal and saved himself $40, even though, in reality, he's still overpaying for the shirt. Although it's the same shirt, consumers are willing to enter the market at different price points because they have placed value on a brand name.

People are obsessed with brand image, and brand image is always tied to price. One of the great things we have been able to do at Universal Windows Direct is to create our brand from scratch. We understood through the process that the stronger our brand was, the more value we would build not just in our company but also in our products and services.

Something else you must understand as a sales professional is the psychology behind the private label. A great example of a private label is Donald Trump. Love him or hate him, even if he does not own a building, once he puts his name on one, people are willing to pay higher rent to live in that building because of its perceived value based on the private label "Trump."

In the appliance industry right now, the majority of all appliances are made in one factory, and three different private-label logos are slapped on them. A consumer will pay more for Maytag if he identifies with the label because his perceived value of those products is that they're reliable (remember the lonely Maytag man with nothing to do?). Going back to the previous chapter on how people buy, private labels differentiate your product or service, making consumers willing to pay more for the same exact product or service.

If you think about this in terms of real estate—in which it's said that location, location, location is everything—people will pay more to be in the Trump building, but they will also pay more to inhabit the building next door, just because it's located nearby. This is a great example of how perceived value or perception of money will drive the consumer to make a decision.

ON THE FLIP SIDE

Now let's flip the discussion: consumers will not buy if the perceived value is not there; they will not want to invest in your product or service.

So in the sales process, there is really no such thing as too much price conditioning.

As a sales technique, we tell our salespeople to start explaining a low-end product versus our highest-end product early in the sales process. Start early and do it often; it's a little like Pavlov's dog—you're going to have almost a conditioned response. For example, if I am in a selling situation and I keep mentioning a $50,000 price tag, I am conditioning the consumer to the perceived value of the product or service.

Another point to keep in mind with price conditioning and perception of value is that where you finish in selling is always relative to where you start. It's a lot harder to sell a product or service by giving a low price and then going up. For example, it's harder to start at $15,000 and go up to $20,000 for a product or service. This, of course, does not mean you cannot offer add-ons to your original sale. But if you want to earn a consumer's business at $12,000, then do not start at $12,000 or they will not feel like they got a good deal.

You can also help with price perception during a sales presentation by using price comparisons. As an expert in your industry, you should know what is going on with your competitors. At Universal Windows Direct, we like to show not only our competitors' prices and comparative value, but we also like to show our prospects third-party information. The Internet is a great tool for locating the cost of anything; there are all kinds of great cost-versus-value reports online, and they're really geared toward helping the consumer to feel comfortable making a decision.

Remember, when you begin a sales situation you're starting at point A, and your job is to take the consumer to point Z. They do not know you, so they do not trust you. They do not want to spend time with you because they do not want to be sold something. They're not sure if they need or want your product because they do not know the offering. They do not have a perception of value or money in mind and you haven't given them a reason to take action yet.

So as it relates to the value discussion, at the beginning of a sales situation, your prospects may:

- have no idea what your product or service costs

- have heard (accurate or not) from a friend or on the Internet what the product or service may cost

- know what they're getting into because you did business with someone they know

COST VERSUS VALUE

It's pretty common for prospects to confuse cost and value. As the sales rep, you must understand that cost is a one-time thing. Cost is today—it's what is incurred by the consumer to do business with you, the sales professional. Value occurs over the life of the product. How long did or will that product last?

Consider a simple example: in my business, rookie sales reps go out and buy the cheapest tape measure available because they think they're going to lose it on the job somewhere. So they spend $10 and within thirty days they haven't lost it, but it breaks and they have to go out and buy another one. If, instead, they had invested a little more in a better-quality tape measure that would last much, much longer, they would experience better average savings over the course of the product's lifetime. Even though the quality product costs more in the beginning, over the product's life it actually gives far more value, costing you less.

In a sales situation, I ask consumers, "Would you rather have a product with a lower cost or a better value?" As I said, cost is easy for a consumer to focus on at that moment: "He's asking me for X amount of dollars," they think. That is real. And it's easy for them to get caught up in paying less for a product, however that product will not last over time.

One of your jobs as a sales professional is to not only justify your cost or the consumer's perception of value but to show the consumer over the product's life how it's going to perform. If you can prove that to consumers, then they're going to be much more likely to pay more for your product or service because you have shown them the value over time. Then, somewhere through the process, the value goes from being perceived to being actual.

BUILDING PERCEIVED VALUE

Earlier, we talked about Upper Level Benefits. In our industry, every window has locks and latches. If my competitors are talking about locks and latches, and I am talking about the safety and security those locks and latches deliver, my product will be of greater value to the consumer. Even though I am presenting in some cases the same feature, I am communicating more value to the consumer. That value proposition can change for the good or bad, based on the prospect's value system, or really, what is in it for them. The further you can drill down and get to what is important to the consumer and make sure that your products and services match those values, the more it's going to be worth for the consumer in value or perceived value.

A great way to communicate this is to have a few buzz phrases that the consumer can tune into. Remember, if you make more than three statements in a row, you lose 50 percent of an adult's attention span. But these three buzz phrases will raise a consumer's antenna because they are about the consumer:

1. "What that means to you is…"

2. "How that benefits you is…"

3. "The advantage to you is…"

It is just human nature to listen when someone is communicating directly about you.

Again, if your competitors are just throwing up features and benefits and not connecting the dots to the value, and you're the one who is going in and really communicating the true end benefit, you are building a tremendous amount of perceived value throughout the process.

It all goes back to the time equation and getting a commitment: you can obviously see it takes more than a few minutes to justify your value proposition. If the consumer does not spend time with you, you cannot build your value.

Another thing to keep in mind is that people buy on the future likelihood of their earning potential, and consumers typically are optimistic. When you think about it, money is not real. Let me explain: My business partner and I wanted to buy a truck. We went to a busy local branch of one of the biggest banks in the world and wanted to withdraw $25,000 of our own money, but the branch did not have enough cash on hand to grant our request (it actually took withdrawals from three branches to get us the full amount). Yet when you pass a bank you think there are millions of dollars sitting in that vault.

When it comes to perception, someone once asked me to think about this: What is the difference between $1 million and $10 million? Most people say $9 million. But what if I draw the numbers out on a whiteboard—$1,000,000 versus $10,000,000? Now look at it again: What's the difference between $10 million and $1 million? The only difference I see is one zero. And what's a zero? A zero is nothing; there's a zero difference between $10 million and $1 million. When you get into business and start making money, you realize none of it actually ends up in your hands. That is the way I was always taught to view money.

That is one of the reasons that I not only love this country but also this profession. When you're exposed to this way of thinking, you get to decide how much income you earn, especially in selling. It's based on how well you prepare but also on how hard you want to work. That is why I love this industry as a whole because it does not matter what you're selling. If you are great at building value, have a good work ethic, and are prepared—because the most prepared salesperson always wins—your income potential is really unlimited.

Another great way to build value is to reintroduce the Thread Technique. Remember, using this technique, we asked the consumer why they were there and what they wanted out of the process. We took the time to write it down. Then we repeated their words to them to clarify.

We talked about how the Thread Technique differentiates you. It really opens up that trust avenue with consumers, which then allows you to attach value to what is important to them. Using the Thread Technique, if the consumer tells me the reason they want to do a home improvement project is to improve the overall look of their home and because they are tired of the maintenance of their current product, my job is to build value by showing them how my product or service is going to fulfill those exact needs. This is a very powerful technique that saves time because you're getting down to the nitty-gritty of what the consumer wants.

If you go into a selling situation and you're presenting a solution that does not match the consumer's wants, needs, and desires, then that solution is not going to have any value to the consumer. Why not do everyone a favor and save a boatload of time and create that thread? And during the product demonstration, be sure you reintroduce the thread, so it has value to the consumer.

Do not forget that you must get a commitment for your product or service. After you have demonstrated your product or service, do not be afraid to ask the consumer if they see the value in it. One way we do this is by sharing third-party information about the average product or service in our marketplace. If we have effectively presented ourselves and our product as above average, then common sense tells the consumer that, if the average price of a product or service in our marketplace is X, then our price should be X-plus because we are above average. If you follow all these techniques that I have shared with you—if you develop trust and invest time with the consumer, if you sharpen the consumer's wants and control the consumer's perception of value or money—then the consumer should see that you're way above average and well worth what you're asking.

The best thing to do after your presentation is to close on the thread. Remind the consumer of what they told you their needs, wants, and desires were, and then ask them if your product or service met or exceeded all those needs, wants, and desires. When they agree to that, they are agreeing that your product or service is valuable and does what they want it to do.

Think of building value as meeting parameters. For example, let's say I decide that I want to go house hunting and my parameters are that the house must have four bedrooms and two-and-a-half baths. It has to be in a specific school system, and it has to be in my price range. Well, if I go out on Saturday and I find a home that meets my parameters, in theory, I should have to buy that home, otherwise I have wasted not only my time, but I have also wasted the Realtor's time. If it does not meet all my parameters—maybe it meets all but one—then it is up to me to decide if I want to compromise my wants, needs, and desires. That is not on the salesperson.

In this scenario, the salesperson (the Realtor) built value by using the Thread Technique to determine what I wanted, and then they made sure the product matched my wants. When you, as a sales rep, build value by meeting all of the consumer's criteria, then it's harder for the consumer to say no.

In fact, your consumers should not only agree that their criteria have been met, but somewhere in the process they should also enter into the hope zone. Remember, this is the place where the consumer gets a little bit nervous and excited because they're not sure they can afford the product. This is good because you want the consumer to wonder whether the product is going to be within their reach. If they do not think it is, then their want level goes through the roof because it's that basic human psychology that we want what we can't have.

If you follow the system I am presenting here—get a commitment on the consumer's time, build trust, fulfill the consumer's needs and wants, and get a commitment on the average price, thus controlling the perception of value—then once the consumer enters into the hope zone, the only thing left to do is present the price options and create some type of urgency, which we're going to cover in the next chapter.

Chapter 8 Takeaways:

- A "good deal" is a state of mind.

- Most people think that money makes the world go 'round. However, in reality, it is the perception of money.

Make It Personal:

- What might prevent your consumers from understanding the value of your products and/or services?

- How do you normally respond when a consumer claims that your product or service is not worth the price you're asking?

- How can you use the Thread Technique to communicate how your product or service will be highly valuable to your consumer based on their wants and needs?

- How can you use third-party information about the products in your market to demonstrate the value of your products and/or services?

CHAPTER 9

CREATE REAL URGENCY

The fifth reason the consumer will or will not buy a product or service is a sense of urgency. This is really the "When" factor.

Urgency is giving a consumer a real reason to take action today. It's a call to action or it's some type of offer. In this chapter, I'll talk about who is using urgency, why it's so important, and how to create real urgency in a selling situation.

I'm sure you have seen this sign hanging in an auto dealership showroom: "The car you looked at today and want to think about and come back and buy tomorrow is the same car that someone looked at yesterday and is coming back to buy today." That sign is reminding the consumer that they had better take action if they want the car they just test drove because yesterday someone went through the same selling process and that consumer has had time to think and is on their way back to purchase the product out from under this consumer.

Employing the "fear of loss" tactic is where most salespeople miss the boat and it is often the most underutilized technique. The reason? Other than the fear of rejection, most salespeople confuse asking for the sale with pressuring someone.

But my father taught me that pressure is just a lack of technique; as a sales rep, if there is pressure in the sales situation, you have not done your job. If you have created a selling situation where all the lights are green—you have invested the time, the consumer likes and trusts you, they understand you have an exclusive product, and you have built value—then asking for the sale should not be a big ordeal. You have to remember that once you have followed the selling process and had all those great commitments along the way, then you need to ask for the sale. You have earned the right to ask for the consumer's business.

PRESSURE IS JUST A LACK OF TECHNIQUE.

Do not confuse asking for the sale with pressure. Again, if you have done a great job of presenting your product, then cost becomes secondary in the process. Consumers will not care what it costs because they want your product or service.

It's hard to believe, but 80 percent of all sales calls end with no attempt by the sales rep to earn the consumer's business. That is a staggering, shocking number. If you're a sales manager or sales professional reading this book, think about how many calls you or your sales reps have made in the last thirty days and how many of them ended by handing the consumer a business card with a pricing proposal and then just walking away.

One of the reasons we're so successful at Universal Windows Direct is because we know this number, but we also know our other numbers. For instance, we know that 80 percent of our sales are made after the fourth or fifth attempt at asking for the business.

This would explain why, in business and in life, the 80/20 rule exists. As that applies to sales, that means that 80 percent of sales are produced by 20 percent of the sales force. Think about it; if eight out of ten sales people are not asking for the business and the other two are, it's no wonder why those two sales reps are superstars. These are the sales reps that don't fear rejection and aren't afraid to ask for the business. In most organizations, two or three sales reps are the bread winners. The rest of the team is in transit; they're either coming in or heading out of the company.

Zig Ziglar calls the rest of these sales reps "professional visitors." They're nice people and they have great product offerings, and their product offering has a great value proposition. But the one thing they're absolutely petrified of is asking for the sale because they want to avoid rejection at all cost.

If you follow the sales system I have laid out for you in this book, you can bust that 80/20 rule. Our organization has tremendous numbers across the nation with all of our salespeople. It's one thing to have one or two great salespeople; it's altogether different to have every single person capable of meeting our industry benchmark of $1.2 million per year, depending on how many appointments they run.

DON'T TAKE REJECTION PERSONALLY

As a sales rep, you must understand that when a consumer says "no," what they really mean is "know." In other words, they're saying, "I don't know enough to take action today." The consumer should feel justified, they should feel like they're getting a good deal, and they should have been given some sort of an incentive to "pull the trigger" on this purchase.

Instead of running away from a "no," you should be empowered by it. The most empowering day of my young sales career was when I was taught that the word "no" was my best friend.

Let's put this whole rejection factor into perspective for a minute. Think back to your eighth-grade dance. You were in the gym. All the girls were on one side of the room, and all the boys were on the other. If you were a guy, the fear wasn't so much of crossing the gym floor and asking a girl to dance. The fear was in what to do if she said no. If that happened, the guy had to walk back across the floor in front of all his buddies and feel like a loser.

So the fear of rejection is learned; this is why creating a sense of urgency is the most underutilized tool in dealing with why a consumer will or will not buy. Too many salespeople are afraid of rejection, or they take it personally.

To close, you must almost take yourself back in time; you must almost become childlike. Just look at a four-year-old who wants something and doesn't understand rejection. They will ask and ask until finally the parent breaks down and gives in to them.

As I mentioned earlier, I have given some pretty exciting presentations over the years, but not once has anyone just handed me their checkbook at the end of the process without me asking for the sale. Even if the consumer loves the product, or they love the service, if I do not ask, then that consumer is going to procrastinate.

One of the reasons you have to ask is because consumers will not retain all the information you gave them. Our presentations can take two or three hours—trust me, that is a lot of information. Within twenty-four to forty-eight hours, the consumer is going to have forgotten 80 to 90 percent of that information. If it takes ten days for me to teach this process to salespeople and many more hours for them to learn it, how can we expect consumers to retain all of the same information when it's told to them inside of two hours? If a prospect tells you they are not comfortable making a decision today, do you really believe that in three weeks after they have forgotten the majority of the information and all they have is a price, that they will then be comfortable going ahead? Not likely.

At Universal Windows Direct, we say, "timid salespeople have skinny children and even skinnier paychecks." You must get over your fear of rejection because you could be the world's greatest person with the world's best intention, but if you do not ask for the consumer's business or sale, you're going to waste everybody's time. In fact, the consumer not only wants you to ask, but they are conditioned and ready for you to ask. So what is stopping you?

WHO UNDERSTANDS URGENCY?

Let me give you some examples of giant corporations that understand the principal of urgency.

To have urgency, you first must have a clock, meaning there has to be some type of original offer with an expiration date. I am always amazed at the consumers who fight this or say, "Oh, this isn't how I do things." But in reality, this is how most transactions in America are done.

In fact, we will use the televised shopping channel QVC as an example. QVC has a clock going when it's offering a product, and it's basically telling you that, "We're offering you this product now, but only for another thirty minutes." In addition to the clock, they have an inventory counter, so they're also informing you that there are, for example, only one hundred Dale Earnhardt commemorative plates left (I think we all know they have a warehouse full of inventory). I like to call this "double urgency"—not only do you have a clock ticking away the time you have remaining to buy, but you also have a limited number of products available, so you must buy now in order to get yours before they're all gone. The techniques work because people get caught up in the fear of loss.

Another example of this is Toyota's annual Toyotathon: "Hurry in. It's the best time to buy." What I do not understand is how Toyota sells cars the rest of the year. What do they do? Do they shut down? Of course not. But once a year, we are all conditioned to that Toyotathon. We all have to run in because that is the best time to buy.

Another great example of creating a sense of urgency is found on eBay, the online auction site. On eBay, you're working against a clock, but you're also doing something unique: you're bidding against other unknown bidders. Like many auctions, online or in person, people tend to pay above market because they get caught up in the bidding process. On eBay, they tend to get caught up in that last thirty seconds because they do not know where the bidding is going to end up, and they're working against the clock.

Even fast-food companies create urgency. Every year, for a limited time, McDonald's brings back the McRib sandwich. Burger King offers limited edition "collectibles" that coincide with movie releases. Chain department stores have President's Day sales. And just look at Black Friday as an example of urgency; people line up in freezing temperatures just to save $99 on a television.

What you're dealing with is a conditioned consumer; they are conditioned to be presented with that sense of urgency. Yes, you may get pushback from some consumers, often because another sales rep has created urgency in a way that placed pressure on the consumer, which really turned them off. But creating urgency is how business is done.

So how do you create urgency?

This goes back to being there for the consumer's needs and wants. If you have fulfilled their needs, wants, and desires, then you have earned the right to ask for the sale. If your urgency strategy includes a discount, rebate, finance program, or other incentive, then that incentive must be absolute: it must end when it's scheduled to end. If you create urgency with an incentive, then you must be willing to stick to your guns that the rebate or discount is only good for this transaction. If you go back on this even one time, then you have cemented in the consumer's mind that you are a liar, and that you will waiver. We call it "the liar once, the liar—period." Now the program is not real and you have just lost all the valuable trust that you have worked so hard to earn.

Whatever type of urgency call you create or use, it must be real and credible, and it must have integrity behind it.

THE BUYING CYCLE

One of the reasons our salespeople have had success is that they understand not only the psychology of How people buy, but also the When. Every consumer is different, and there is a threshold that I like to call "the buying cycle."

We know that 80 percent of our sales are made after the fourth or fifth time we ask a consumer to earn their business. I go into one person's home and they may say "no" to me four times. I go into another person's home and they may say "yes" to me right off the rip. Another person may never say "yes" to me. Consumers are impulsive. That is the reality of the job. No matter what kind of offer I make or what kind of effort I put forth, they may never buy.

So the buying cycle I am going to discuss begins once you have presented the consumer with an initial price that is good for a set amount of time.

In the old days, we were taught, "Just present your price and wait for the consumer to talk first. Whoever talks first loses." Well, I believe that way of thinking is a tremendous waste of time. When I present my initial price, which is good for a full thirty days, then I am going to ask for the consumer's business right away. In this scenario, I am assuming the consumer wants to buy from me; keep in mind that the most powerful close is the assumptive close.

Now the reason I assume they want to buy is because I believe I did my job, and I believe in my company and my product. So I present the price and I ask for the sale. I do not waste any time whatsoever. I know more than likely the consumer is going to say "no" to me. But that is okay because I know it's coming, and I am empowered.

Once I get that "no," then I give the consumer some type of new information, which may be finance options or terms. In selling, when we give a prospect new information, we're able to ask for a new decision. Once I have given that new information, I ask for the business again. The objective is to get another "no" out of the way in order to keep moving toward the sale. Remember, the majority of sales are made after four or five "nos."

The consumer may say, "I'm still not ready. It still doesn't fit. I need time to think about it." I am okay with that. There is no problem whatsoever in that scenario. But the new information I presented justifies my re-asking for the business. This is where most salespeople get creamed because they do not know how to present that new information without it coming across as high pressure. That is not the goal. Again, we want this to be a fun, easy process during which we both win.

> IN SELLING, WHEN WE GIVE A PROSPECT NEW INFORMATION, WE'RE ABLE TO ASK FOR A NEW DECISION.

The way to manage the mood of the situation is through voice inflection and body language, which I talked about earlier. This is where it's important to stay in control of your faculties. When you're presenting your product or service, you're standing tall, you're leaning forward, you're excited. You're putting on a show. But when you're asking for someone's business, you really want to slow your pace, lower your tone, lean back.

Remember also that humor is your friend here. Keep the tempo light and moving. This is a differentiator; when it comes time to ask for the wallet, the consumer will tense up. So instead of being in the consumer's face, lighten up. Do not take the situation too seriously. Remember, the consumer will be your best friend until you start asking for money. So sometimes in a closing situation, it's about making the consumer feel comfortable enough to say "yes" to you.

For instance, if the consumer says "no" to the finance options, that is okay. "No problem." Now it's time to appeal to their logical side; all along, we have been appealing to their emotional side because we know that people buy emotionally, and they justify it logically. In a good selling system, after you have presented your price and received a "no," and then you have presented new information such as finance options and received a "no," then you should have some type of logical return on investment close to present to the consumer.

All products and services have some form of payback or return on investment in some form or fashion.

In our business, it's very easy for us to show a consumer through resale value, increased equity, and energy savings that windows are free. Beyond free, they actually put money back in the consumer's pocket.

If you can demonstrate some type of return on investment proposition to the consumer, then you are giving them new information, you are appealing to the logical side of the brain, and you are helping them reach the ultimate justification.

Usually, we ask for the business twice while discussing return on investment. If the consumer still says "no," then you must go through the qualification process. This process will determine what type of call to action or urgency needs to be presented.

QUALIFYING THE PROSPECT

Having received several "nos" from the consumer, before creating an urgency call by offering a discount, you must pause and qualify your prospect. This involves asking a series of questions to ensure that the consumer even deserves to have the urgency call or the discount offered.

How do you do that? Start by asking about his or her time frame for buying. Typically, that time frame is going to be for however long your original offer is good. For example, you might say, "Just to clarify, you're in the market to do this project or buy this product within the next thirty days?" If they can't get back to you within the time frame that your original price is good, then you should not offer the discount because they're not a qualified consumer. If the consumer says "yes," that is the first green light, and it makes good business sense to give them an incentive to get them to take action today.

Next, qualify the consumer by ensuring that they're actually planning to invest in the project: "In that time frame, this is something you're definitely going to do?" If the consumer says "yes" to this question, they have committed that they are indeed planning to buy.

Then, simply ask the consumer if they like working with you, if they like your company, and if they feel your product is quality. If the consumer says yes, that is another qualifier.

If you really think about what we're doing here, you have already received these commitments through the presentation. We're just reiterating and re-qualifying— reminding the consumer that this is where we are in the process. This part of the process is also about getting the consumer to hear their own commitment. You want the consumer to hear themself say: "Yes, I'm acting in the next thirty days. Yes, I'm doing this project. Yes, I like you. Yes, I like your company. Yes, I love your product."

When you have all these commitments except the most important one, then you must ask, "What's the one thing stopping us from coming together today?" "It sounds like the only thing stopping me from earning your business is the money; it's the money isn't it?" Typically, we want to isolate objections down to one (which is always the money), otherwise the consumer tends to jump like a bullfrog to different lily pads. If they give you three different objections and you cover one, then they will jump to the next objection; you cover that one, and they jump to the next; and it just keeps going. In this scenario, it's nearly impossible to close without isolating the single real objection.

As part of the qualifying process, you must get the consumer to commit to committing. In this scenario, we ask them another set of questions where we basically eliminate the "maybe." Now, if you take a look at any selling situation, the consumer at the end can say one of three things to a salesperson. They can say "yes," which is great. We love hearing "yes." They could say "no." Or they could say "maybe."

"Maybe" can come in many different forms. It can sound like, "Well, I'll get back to you," or, "I'd like to talk to other companies," or, "I need to sleep on it." "Maybe" is a nice, polite way to say "no." If I can get the consumer to commit to a "yes" or "no" upon my initial presentation, I have just eliminated the "maybe." When I eliminate the "maybe," the consumer is giving me a definite answer. One thing I know from experience is that it's the "maybes" that will drive a salesperson crazy, if not run them out of selling altogether.

This is huge in the sales process. Let's look at it mathematically: If we were to draw this out on a whiteboard, in percentages, the "yes, no, maybe" equation is equal parts 33, 33, and 33 percent. If you eliminate the "maybe," you're down to 50/50 percent. The probability actually tips in your favor 52/48 percent.

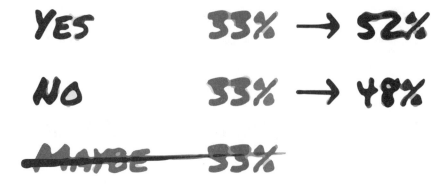

By learning how to get the consumer to commit to committing, or eliminating the "maybe," you are increasing your odds of selling dramatically. You still will not be able to sell everybody, but you will be able to sell more.

Let's say this helps you sell 20 percent more. If you're running ten sales calls a week and you're 20 percent better, you're talking about 104 more sales a year. That truly is the difference between being a top earner and an average earner.

PRESENTING THE DISCOUNT

Using my sales system, you will ask for the business at least three or four times at the original price. For all intents and purposes, when you present the discount, you're in that fourth or fifth attempt where 80 percent of sales are made. The only thing you have not done is create that sense of urgency or give the consumer a reason to take action.

Here is why it's important to ask for the business several times before offering a discount: the reason closing has gotten a bad name is because the untrained or lazy sales rep presents the consumer with a price, and when they get a "no," they then take out their magic wand and start slashing the price.

But if you go from $10,000 to $9,000 to $8,000, two things are going to happen. First, you're going to lose credibility with the consumer, and second, that consumer is going to wonder how low you could have gone. The worst thing you can do is create a selling scenario where the consumer is left wondering. Remember, a good deal is a state of mind, and you want your consumer to know they got a great deal.

> THE WORST THING YOU CAN DO IS CREATE A SELLING SCENARIO WHERE THE CONSUMER IS LEFT WONDERING.

So what is a good discount? Well, one that works, but more importantly one that is justified and real. Whatever the discount, if it is not presented properly, you can do more harm than good. All that trust and credibility that you built will be forgotten immediately if the consumer begins to feel uncomfortable at this point. If you give too small of a discount, then you can run the risk of the prospect not feeling enough urgency. If you give too big of a discount too fast, it may not be believable and you lose credibility. It's over.

You must present the consumer with some type of mutually beneficial incentive to make it a win-win. Remember that, just like the consumer, your most valuable resource is time. So a mutually beneficial win is one where the consumer helps you as well. Salespeople incur real costs every day; every repeat visit you make to a consumer costs you money and ultimately lowers your success rate.

Typically, a 10 to 18 percent discount based on the opportunity cost is a pretty fair number. It's believable. It's real. And it's really what it costs you to miss the opportunity in front of you.

When you present the discount, you want to assume that the consumer is ready to buy because you have just gone through a selling system where all five psychological reasons that the consumer would or wouldn't buy have been covered, including a call to action.

Remember, the consumer is conditioned. They have had an urgent reason to purchase everything they have bought, from their fast food to their home. At this point, you are at the threshold; here, it's okay for you to feel uncomfortable, but it's not okay for the consumer to feel uncomfortable.

The whole goal is to do this entire sales process tactfully. Never use pressure. You are there to earn the consumer's business, and even if you do not earn their business, you want to leave every sales call gracefully and thankfully. Always thank consumers for their time because they have invested time with you, whether they purchase or not. They did a respectful thing; they let you go from A to Z. They let you go through the selling process, which is your job. But if you have truly done your job, more often than not, the consumer is going to buy from you because you have presented a solution to a problem that they needed or wanted solved.

Chapter 9 Takeaways:

The Buying Cycle:

- Present a price (get a "no").

- Present new information (get a "no").

- Present R.O.I. (get two more "nos").

- Qualify the consumer.

- Isolate the process to one objection.

- Eliminate the "maybe."

- Get a commitment to commit.

- Present a discount.

Make It Personal:

- What would motivate your consumers to change their response from "maybe" to "yes"?

- What types of expiration dates can you include with your offers and incentives to create a sense of urgency?

- Are you offering discounts too quickly? How can you improve the way in which you use discounts to incentivize the sale?

CHAPTER 10

FORGE YOUR OWN PATH

In 2008, my business partner and I almost bought into the recession. We would go to trade shows and industry events, and everywhere there was doom and gloom. Talks of downsizing and advertising budget cuts were rampant among other industry leaders. We got word that two of our major competitors were talking about not only cutting their advertising budgets, but they were also planning to lay off some talented people. I was taught that the difference between a recession and a depression was that in a recession, your neighbor is out of work, and in a depression you are out of work! So we knew from experience that this recession was going to be as good or as bad as our participation level in it.

Up until that point, we had never really had an advertising budget like our major competitors. We were relatively a mom-and-pop shop that practiced hard-core guerilla marketing—going door to door to generate low-cost leads and using trade shows and events to effectively generate additional leads.

During this time, we had a company meeting and we communicated to our team that, no matter what's going on outside our doors, they were to focus only on our positive growth and the other positive pieces of our business.

Instead of focusing on 10 percent unemployment, as the media did, we chose to focus on 90 percent employment! Zig Ziglar said, business is not good or bad out there, it's good or bad in here. That "in here" is the space between your ears.

So we were blessed. As individuals, we had been exposed to thinking differently about challenges. The word "crisis" truly can have many meanings, but it's all in how we approach it. Where others saw obstacles, we saw opportunity.

In a very counterintuitive move, when others cut back on advertising, we gambled and quadrupled our footprint. It all started at a local trade show here in Cleveland, Ohio.

Normally, we would be in a small ten-by-ten-foot booth with basic samples. We invested our last dollars in a twenty-by-twenty-foot space with all brand-new samples. We looked good, and we were ready to recover from a rough winter. We had to have a great first quarter, so we put everything we had into this upcoming show. Looking back, it was one of those watershed moments for our company. We bet on ourselves when others were betting on failure.

I'll never forget the opening day of that show because we got hit with a terrible snowstorm and attendance was way off. My partner, Mike Strmac, and I looked at each other and thought, "Great, we just invested our last dollars, and the opening day was a disaster." Everything was on the line.

But the weather broke the next morning and we generated four times the sales calls we had from the same show the previous year! We parlayed that victory into a mass media television and radio campaign. Once again, we went way outside of our comfort zone, investing the equivalent of what we would spend in an entire year into a single month.

The results were astonishing. We not only had an explosion of growth, but we also took valuable market share from our competitors who had their heads in the sand. One major, well-known household competitor went out of business altogether. We have never relinquished this market share and we never will.

In an earlier chapter, I discussed why the majority of people are negative. It's easy to be negative and follow everyone else off the cliff. There is a difference between jumping off a cliff and taking a leap of faith. Misery truly loves company. The best part is you get to decide whether or not to participate!

Most hyper-successful people make their money by going against the grain, not with it. Success, like positivity, is a choice. Do not let outside factors affect how you operate and plan for the future. Plan for success and have faith that you will achieve what you focus on.

This counterintuitive nature has served me well throughout my career. Not following the crowd does have its benefits. One of the major benefits is capitalizing on the opportunities that others missed while they are participating in the status quo.

IT'S NOT FOR EVERYBODY

The great sales trainer Dave Yoho taught me the three basic things that a human being will avoid at all costs: being alone, being in an uncomfortable situation, and rejection. These three things are what keep people complacent, preventing personal and professional growth.

#1 AVOIDANCE:
BEING ALONE

The first thing a person will avoid at all cost is being alone. We may think we want to be alone or need some alone time, but at the end of the day, we all want to be a part of something. We want to be a part of a tribe, a pack, or even a gang.

Think about the phenomenon of college and professional sports. People go nuts during the professional football season for their NFL home team. Americans spend billions of dollars a year on apparel, tickets, and fantasy football, etc.

As an example, I am a season ticketholder and a diehard Cleveland Browns fan. In my years as a fan I have endured embarrassing one-win seasons. The organization has never gone to a Super Bowl since its inception! They even had the audacity to relocate the team to Baltimore, even though we have one of the most loyal fan bases in the world. I was devastated.

So why would someone endure being a Cleveland Browns fan? The answer is a shared identity. I can be at the San Francisco International Airport and see another guy wearing a Browns hat, and even though I do not know that person, I can identify with him. He's just as miserable and as frustrated of a fan as I am. A strength-in-numbers mentality kicks in and we feel like we are in it together. Not only can I identify with him, but I can strike up a conversation with this complete stranger about how bad we botched this year's draft again.

#2 AVOIDANCE: BEING PUT INTO AN UNCOMFORTABLE OR UNFAMILIAR SITUATION

The second thing we all want to avoid is being put into a new or uncomfortable situation. Ask yourself what people fear more: shark attacks or public speaking? Most people fear public speaking way more than sharks. Have you ever had to address a crowd? It is a daunting task. Think of the John Quinones's show *What Would Do You?*—a hidden camera show that puts people in really uncomfortable situations. Even when a person knows someone is misbehaving, they will not speak up the majority of the time to avoid an uncomfortable interaction.

#3 AVOIDANCE: REJECTION

People are petrified of rejection; they avoid it like the plague. This fear of rejection is why the majority of all sales calls end with no attempt at asking for the sale. Salespeople take rejection personally, and it makes them uncomfortable.

A child is not afraid of rejection until rejection is learned. Think of a three-year-old who wants something; he will ask and ask until he gets his way. Children have no fear of rejection, which is why they're great salespeople. As a canvasser going door-to-door, I learned how to handle rejection on a massive scale. This experience shaped my entrepreneurial destiny.

One of the reasons sales is one of the highest paid professions in the world is we ask salespeople to deal with all three of these things—being alone, being in an uncomfortable situation, and rejection—on a daily basis.

> YOU CAN MAKE EXCUSES OR YOU CAN MAKE MONEY, BUT YOU CAN'T MAKE BOTH.

Think about this: typically, even if you're part of a sales team, your results are your own. At the end of a month or quarter, the sales board does not lie. The numbers you post are yours and yours alone. You cannot hide. I always tell my sales representatives, "You can make excuses or you can make money, but you can't make both." You're absolutely the master of your own destiny; you're alone in this process.

My father taught me that, no matter how well your last thirty days went, we all start over on the first day of the month. We wipe the slate clean and our focus must shift onto the present. So, not only are we alone as sales professionals, but we're asked to go into new situations every day.

There is some basic truth to the fact that people are people. But in my experience, no two selling situations are ever identical. You have different types of personalities and you never know what kind of mood you may catch your prospect in. We all want to catch them after they learned they got a bonus at work, but it does not always work out that way. The key is to treat each new situation with enthusiasm and respect regardless of the circumstance.

So you're alone, you're being put in new situations each day, and oh, by the way, you're going to be asked to handle rejection on a massive scale gracefully.

All three things are against the grain and are counterintuitive to what feels right. Welcome to the world of selling.

The day I was taught that, in selling, the word "no" is not my enemy but my friend was an empowering day. Instead of running away from it, I was taught to run at it and get it out of the way.

Let's also not forget that one of the keys to "How" consumers buy is to be different. If the majority of salespeople are not asking for the order at all, then there can be nothing more different than someone asking for the order five or six times! If you grasp this concept and hold yourself accountable, this is what is in it for you: an above-average existence with above-average earning potential. I believe if you're willing to do something others are not willing to do you should get compensated highly. You're empowered and you should be proud of your profession, no matter what you sell.

SKILL VERSUS WILL

We often debate whether great salespeople are born or made. That is to say: Is being a great salesperson more about skill, or more about will, or is it a combination of both? As I mentioned earlier, there is an old joke that goes like this: A tourist asks a New Yorker how to get to Carnegie Hall. The New Yorker replies, "Practice!" The same holds true in sales. Remember, the amount of energy you put into something will be in direct proportion to what you get out of it.

When I interview potential candidates for a sales position, they all say, "I want to make lots of money." Understand this: the only people who make money work at the United States Mint. The rest of us have to earn money. How you earn money is to be of service to your prospects, your friends, and your family. The more service you provide, the more money you earn. If you want to earn more, you must be of more service to the people around you, and your return for this service always comes back to you. Sometimes, it comes back from somewhere other than where you spread it, but it comes back, nevertheless. Understanding this concept and committing to being of service is paramount in living a purposeful, fulfilled life.

If you test a potential sales rep on the standard DISC Personality Test, you are measuring where they fall in four categories—you're looking to see what their natural-born abilities are.

We always look for a combination of a highly dominant and highly influential personality. These same people will score low in the compliant and supportive areas of the test.

There is some truth to the fact that you're born with a certain amount of aptitude to become a great salesperson. I always say I can teach a person how to sell, but they either have the *hutzpah* to ask for the sale or they don't. Show me the amount of rejection someone is willing to take, and I'll show you how much money they're going to make.

> SHOW ME THE AMOUNT OF REJECTION SOMEONE IS WILLING TO TAKE, AND I'LL SHOW YOU HOW MUCH MONEY THEY'RE GOING TO MAKE.

One of the reasons I set out to write this book was to empower and help sales professionals understand the "When" someone buys in the buying cycle. If you're empowered and understand that having the consumer object and say "no" is just part of the process, then the process comes down to how much tenacity and drive you have when asking for the sale.

One of my favorite closes I use in a home is my Belief Close. This close is used when the consumer thinks you're being a little aggressive. Remember pressure is a lack of technique and poise. Here is an example:

> *Mr. Prospect, if you had a sales rep in your home who did a three-hour presentation and at the end he didn't ask for the sale, that would tell you one of three things about that salesperson: One, he doesn't believe in his product or it won't perform the way he's promised; two, he doesn't believe in the price, or it's not fairly priced in the marketplace; or three, he doesn't believe in himself and the company he works for. I have to ask, is that the type of person you would feel comfortable investing with?*

> *It may seem like I'm pushing a bit right now, and I am. The reason I am is because I believe in my product and how it*

will benefit your life. I believe my product is fairly priced in the marketplace. And, most importantly, I believe in my company and myself. You believe in me, don't you? And isn't that the type of company, product, and person you want to buy from—one you believe in?

Great, let's get you rolling because you're already believing. (Put a huge goofy smile on your face, nod your head up and down, and stick out your hand.)

DO THE MATH

Here is a great example of a willing salesperson asking for the sale with a smile. I also like to look at being successful in sales as a mathematical equation. If I have fifty salespeople who are, on average, asking prospects for their business five more times than my competition, at two sales calls a day, six days a week for fifty-two weeks, that's 156,000 more attempts made per year than my competition makes. With that many more attempts, common sense says we're going to have a higher success rate than anyone in the industry.

I have come to the conclusion that being a great salesperson is truly a combination of both skill and will. Give me the willing, and they can develop the skill over time.

Think about that poignant conversation I had with my father when I got bounced out of The Ohio State University. He made me promise that if I was going down this path as a salesman, that I wouldn't be a hack. A hack is someone who does not take the profession of selling seriously, a lazy salesperson who does not commit the extra time to prepare and perfect their craft. I like to consider the sales profession as an ever-expanding educational experience that never stops. I challenge you to make this same commitment and see where it takes you.

Chapter 10 Takeaways:

Three Basic Things a Human Being Will Avoid at All Costs:

- Being alone

- Being in an uncomfortable situation

- Rejection

These three things keep people complacent and prevent personal and professional growth.

Make It Personal:

- In what ways are you complacent?

- How might your fears be holding you back from greatness?

- What dreams or ideas are you ignoring due to fear? How can you overcome your fear to stand out from the pack?

CONCLUSION

PREPARED AND PERSISTENT

I ventured out with a designated purpose. The purpose was to write a book that would not only add value to sales professionals' careers but would also change their perspective on the possibilities in life. One of the reasons I am passionate about training salespeople is that every selling situation can be an education in itself.

In the process of writing this book, I learned a lot about myself. I had a lot of doubt and fear creep in. I worried about having enough relative content. I worried about how it would turn out and how my peers would perceive it.

In short, I found myself way outside of my comfort zone. Once that discomfort set in, I knew I was on the right track. I got excited about feeling doubt; it motivated me, and I realized I needed to take my own advice as well as the advice of some of my favorite thinkers of our time.

Personal development personality Earl Nightingale teaches that fear and worry are wasted emotions. They will cripple you and prevent you from attempting great things. William Shakespeare said doubt and fear are often traitors of our mind that prevent us from achieving success. I stayed persistent and worked at this project with my goal not only in mind but also in front of me on paper. I believe that had I not written out the goal of writing this with a purpose, I would have never finished it. Persistence is another word for faith. Having faith and purpose is powerful. If you discover your purpose and have faith, anything is possible.

Persistence in selling is another way for you to declare that you have faith in yourself and your product. When you have this belief system, pushy sales tactics are replaced with persistent sales tactics.

Remember, the most prepared salespeople win. You are now empowered. You know Why, How, and When prospects buy. You can go into any selling situation and operate with a calm, cool demeanor. I love the saying "Desperation is a stinky cologne"; the consumer can smell it a mile away. But you cannot miss if you create a sales process designed around the five following things:

- Time: With time, you can build value in your product or service.

- Trust (the most important): Over half of the equation is your likability and believability.

- Need/Want/Hope: Sharpen the consumer's want level with a Unique Selling Position (USP)—even if the USP is you!

- Perception of Value: Create a good value proposition by controlling the perceived value of your product or service.

- Urgency (the most underutilized): Create a real reason for the prospect to take action now. Make it a win-win proposition.

Create a sales process where all five reasons are covered, and the prospect will have no choice but to buy from you.

Keep in mind that the best way to cover an objection is to bring it up first. This allows you to stay in control and cover any concerns before they arise. This is a proactive sales approach versus a reactive one.

If you do not have a written goal or purpose prior to reading this book, I highly suggest you meditate on one immediately. Take the time to ask yourself what you want out of life. If you do have a goal, I suggest you revisit it and ask yourself if you're aiming high enough.

Remember, the definition of success as I have come to understand it is having a worthwhile, written purpose with precise dates that you are presently working toward. The moment you decide to achieve something, you are a success. The best part is you do not even have to understand how to accomplish something—you just have to want it enough. A great example is the writing of this book. I had no idea how to write a book or any resources to do so when I started. I had a written goal and an outline. What I really had was faith and purpose—the rest took care of itself.

In loving memory of our faithful companion,
Scout Barr

August 1, 2005—September 2, 2016

ABOUT UNIVERSAL WINDOWS DIRECT

Universal Windows Direct was founded in April 2002 by William H. Barr III and Michael Strmac of Fairview Park, Ohio. It was their mission to create a home improvement company that offers high-quality home improvement goods at the best market value. What began as two guys in a 300-square-foot office quickly grew to become one of the nation's leading remodeling companies.

Today, Universal Windows Direct represents thousands of customers and has a rapidly growing dealer network with locations nationwide, all of which are actively involved in the communities they serve.

For Dealership and Franchise Opportunities

(Exclusive territories are going fast!)

Inquire at

www.yourwindowopportunity.com

or contact

Universal Windows Direct
Dealer Development

216-518-8900

For Training and Coaching Availability

including

Keynote Addresses

Lead Generation
Canvassing as well as Shows and Events

Sales Training
Developing a Unique Sales Position
Presentation Development
Qualifying and Closing

Coaching
Setting and Achieving Goal Sessions
Individual and Group.

Inquire at

www.williamhbarr.com

216-509-2101

Prices and availability upon request